# THE KETO DIET COOKBOOK

# 550

Easy & Healthy Ketogenic Diet Recipes, 21-Day Meal Plan, Lose Up To 20 Pounds In 3 Weeks.

BY

Francis Michael

## COPYRIGHT © 2020 by Francis Michael

**ISBN: 978-1-952504-09-9**

All rights reserved. This book is copyright protected and it's for personal use only. Without the prior written permission of the publisher, no part of this publication should be reproduced, distributed, or transmitted in any form or by any means, including photocopying, recording, or other electronic or mechanical methods. This publication is sold with the idea that the publisher is not required to render accounting, officially permitted, or otherwise, qualified services. Seek for the services of a legal or professional, a practiced individual in the profession if advice is needed.

## DISCLAIMER

The information contained in this book is geared for educational and entertainment purposes only. Strenuous efforts have been made towards providing accurate, up to date and reliable complete information. The information in this book is true and complete to the best of our knowledge. Neither the publisher nor the author takes any responsibility for any possible consequences of reading or enjoying the recipes in this book. The author and publisher disclaim any liability in connection with the use of information contained in this book. Under no circumstance will any legal responsibility or blame be apportioned against the author or publisher for any reparation, damages, or monetary loss due to the information herein, either directly or indirectly.

## Table of Contents

INTRODUCTION .................................................................... 11

Meaning of Keto Diet ............................................................ 11

How Keto Diet Works ........................................................... 12

Benefits of Keto Diet ............................................................ 13

How to Kick-Start Ketosis .................................................... 14

Meaning of Carbs ................................................................. 15

Foods That Are High On Carbs ............................................ 16

Foods to Eat on Keto Diet .................................................... 17

Foods To Avoid on Keto Diet ............................................... 18

Smart Tips to Achieve Success On Keto Diet ..................... 19

Smart Tips for Eating Out on Keto Diet ............................. 20

## SMOOTHIE & BREAKFAST RECIPES ................. 21

Green Smoothie .......................................................................... 21

Chocolate Fat Bomb Smoothie ................................................. 22

Breakfast Pizza ........................................................................... 23

Golden Smoothie ........................................................................ 24

Iced Matcha Latte ....................................................................... 25

Mocha Smoothie ......................................................................... 26

CBD Rooibos Tea Latte .............................................................. 27

Milkshake Smoothie with Raspberries ................................... 28

Flu Smoothie ............................................................................... 29

Breakfast Egg Crepes ................................................................. 30

Coffee Smoothie ................................................................................. 31

Frosted Vanilla Blackberry Lemonade ............................................. 32

Chocolate Peanut Butter Smoothie ................................................. 33

Salted Caramel Smoothie ................................................................ 34

Coconut Milk Strawberry Smoothie ................................................ 35

Buttery Coconut Flour Waffles ....................................................... 36

Coconut Chia Smoothies ................................................................. 37

Fruit-Free Smoothie ........................................................................ 38

Avocado Smoothie with Coconut Milk, Ginger, and Turmeric . 39

Blueberry Protein Power Smoothie ................................................ 40

Mocha Smoothie .............................................................................. 41

Matcha Green Tea Smoothie .......................................................... 42

Fluffy Almond Flour Pancakes ....................................................... 43

Mint Coco Smoothie ....................................................................... 44

Cinnamon Chocolate Breakfast Smoothie .................................... 45

## BRUNCH & DINNER RECIPES ............................................. 46

French Toast Sticks ......................................................................... 46

Raspberry Cheesecake Bars ............................................................ 47

Chia Jam ........................................................................................... 48

Raspberry Linzer Cookie Bars ....................................................... 49

Lemon Poppy Seed Donuts ........................................................... 50

Blueberry Jam .................................................................................. 52

Cappuccino Muffins ........................................................................ 53

Strawberry Scones ........................................................................... 55

Pistachio Shortbread Cookies ........................................................ 56

Cherry Clafoutis..................................................................57

Blueberry Pancake Bites...................................................58

Almond Crescent Cookies ................................................60

Cloud Bread Cheese Danish .............................................61

Pistachio Truffles Fat Bombs ............................................62

Avocado Egg .......................................................................63

Baked Denver Omelet .......................................................64

# POULTRY RECIPES..........................................................65

Golden Chicken Bacon Fritter Balls.................................65

Chicken Tenders.................................................................66

Garlic Bacon Wrapped Chicken Bites .............................67

Chicken and Bacon Sausages ...........................................68

Chicken, Bacon, and Apple Mini Meatloaves ................69

Crispy Baked Buffalo Wings .............................................70

Tandoori Chicken Wings with Mint Chutney ................71

Grilled Cilantro Lime Chicken Wings .............................73

Chicken Bulgogi with Sesame Garnish ...........................74

Asian Chicken Thighs........................................................75

Chicken Massaman Curry with Daikon Radishes.........76

Caprese Hasselback Chicken............................................77

Chicken Korma ..................................................................78

Bruschetta Chicken ...........................................................80

Chicken Divan Casserole..................................................82

Pecan Crusted Chicken.....................................................83

Chicken Club Lettuce Wraps ...........................................84

## SOUP, STEW & SALAD RECIPES ........................... 85

   Chicken Enchilada Soup ............................................................... 85

   Chicken and Cabbage Stew ......................................................... 86

   Chicken "Ramen" Soup ................................................................ 87

   Homemade Thai chicken broth ................................................... 88

   Chicken Noodle Soup .................................................................. 89

   Chicken Fajita Soup ..................................................................... 90

   Asian Miso Soup Topped with Shrimp ....................................... 92

   Salmon Stew ................................................................................. 93

   Simple Coconut Seafood Soup .................................................... 94

   Spicy Halibut Tomato Soup ........................................................ 95

   Creamy Leek & Salmon Soup ..................................................... 96

   Thai Coconut Soup with Shrimp ................................................. 97

   Cheesy Zucchini Soup ................................................................. 98

   Cabbage Soup .............................................................................. 99

   Spring Soup with Poached Egg ................................................. 100

   Mint Avocado Chilled Soup ...................................................... 101

   Thai Beef and Broccoli Soup .................................................... 102

   Turmeric Bone Broth ................................................................. 103

   Bacon Cheeseburger Soup ........................................................ 104

## BEEF & PORK RECIPES ............................................. 105

   Pork Egg Roll in A Bowl .......................................................... 105

   Bacon Covered Meatloaf .......................................................... 106

   Spaghetti Squash with Meat Sauce .......................................... 107

Ground Pork Tacos ............................................................... 108

Homemade "Hungarian" Sausage ........................................ 109

Pork and Cashew Stir-Fry ..................................................110

Chili Beef ............................................................................111

Pan-Fried Pork Tenderloin ................................................. 112

Cheesy Mexican Taco Skillet .............................................. 113

Mu Shu Pork ...................................................................... 114

Spicy Pork with Kelp Noodles ............................................ 115

Apple Dijon Pork Chops .................................................... 116

Pork Chops & Cabbage ...................................................... 117

Korean Ground Beef Stir Fry ............................................. 118

Cajun pork with Peppers and Tomatoes ............................ 120

Dry Rub Pork Spare Ribs ................................................... 121

Cheeseburger Meatloaf.......................................................122

Jamaican Jerk Pork Roast...................................................123

San Choy Bau......................................................................124

Beef Cheeks.........................................................................125

# FISH & SEAFOOD RECIPES ......................................126

Steamed Clams ...................................................................126

Spicy Mussels in Tomato Chorizo Broth............................127

Garlic Lemon Butter Crab Legs..........................................128

Soft Shell Crab....................................................................129

Salmon in Foil Packets with Pesto......................................130

Salmon Roasted in Butter .................................................. 131

Grilled Salmon with Creamy Pesto Sauce..........................132

Cajun Salmon Patties .................................................................. 133

Grilled Swordfish Skewers ......................................................... 134

Almond and Parmesan Crusted Fish ....................................... 135

Thai Seafood Chowder ............................................................... 136

Hazelnut Crusted Sea Bass....................................................... 138

Buttered Cod in Skillet ............................................................... 139

Fried Fish....................................................................................... 140

Tuna Melts ................................................................................... 141

# VEGETERIAN & VEGAN RECIPES ................... 142

Smoothie Bowl............................................................................. 142

Maple Oatmeal ........................................................................... 143

Keto Guacamole ......................................................................... 144

Low Carb Crackers ..................................................................... 145

Avocado Arugula Tomato Salad .............................................. 146

Triple Green Kale Salad............................................................. 147

Tomato Mushroom Spaghetti Squash .................................... 149

Ginger Asian Slaw ....................................................................... 150

Roasted Cauliflower Soup ......................................................... 151

Ginger Cauliflower Fried Rice.................................................... 152

Garlic Roasted Radishes............................................................ 153

Roasted Cabbage with Lemon ................................................. 154

Garlic Aioli .................................................................................... 155

Homemade Vegan Ranch ......................................................... 156

Basil Pesto .................................................................................... 157

Chocolate Almond Avocado Pudding.................................... 158

## APPETIZER RECIPES ............................................................159
   Veggie Dip..........................................................................159
   Chicken Wings ................................................................. 160
   Macadamia Nut Hummus ............................................... 161
   Spicy Cheese Crisps .........................................................162
   Antipasto Kebabs...............................................................163
   Jalapeno Poppers ..............................................................164
   Keto Meatballs ..................................................................165
   Brown Butter Buffalo Bites .............................................166
   Baked Sea Scallops ...........................................................167
   Broccoli Casserole ............................................................169
   Bacon Wrapped Brussel Sprouts ....................................170
   Naruto Rolls ...................................................................... 171
   Crab Cake...........................................................................172
   Roasted Salt & Pepper Radish Chips .............................173
   Black Olive Tapenade .......................................................174
   Cucumber Salsa ................................................................175
   Creamy Avocado Sauce ...................................................176

## DESSERT RECIPES ...............................................................177
   Blueberry Cupcakes..........................................................177
   Flourless Chocolate Cake ................................................178
   No-Bake Coconut Cookies...............................................179
   Coconut Macaroons ........................................................ 180
   Shortbread Cookies ..........................................................181

Coconut Lime Bars ..................................................................... 183

Coconut Blondies ...................................................................... 185

Chocolate Coconut Bars ........................................................... 186

Vanilla Bean Ice Cream ............................................................ 187

Avocado Popsicles ................................................................... 188

Frozen Fudge Pops .................................................................. 189

Strawberry Ice Cream ............................................................. 190

Raspberry Lemon .................................................................... 191

Pots De Creme ......................................................................... 192

Chocolate Mousse ................................................................... 193

Coffee Panna Cotta .................................................................. 195

Lemon Coconut Custard Pie ................................................... 196

# 21-Day Meal Plan To Lose Up To 20 Pounds In 3 Weeks ................................................................. 197

# INTRODUCTION

## Meaning of Keto Diet

When talking about Keto Diet, it's simply a short form for Ketogenic Diet. The diet has to do much with a low-carb (carbohydrate) meal. This means the process of lowering intake of carbohydrates and increasing the intake of fat. This leads to fat being turn into ketones. The Ketones in turn supplies the human brain with energy. It also involves much intake of fats, veggies and proteins etc. Keto Diet however helps to burn fats instead of burning carbohydrates. Carbohydrates are converted into glucose which in turn helps to energies the human brain. If small amount of carbohydrates are contain in a particular diet, the liver converts fat into fatty acids and ketone bodies.

## How Keto Diet Works

In reality, Keto Diet places it emphases on fat which make up to about 95%nof daily calories. The human body in the other hand makes use of different types of fuel for its healthy living. The keto Diet is capable of providing the human body diverse kinds of fuel. This fuel is known as Ketone. The Liver uses stored fat to manufacture this Ketone. The Keto Diet works perfectly well if one follows it instructions properly. The Keto Diet in the other hand needs you to deny yourself intake of carbohydrates. Reaching A state called Ketosis may take some few days but this can be interfered when you consume too much protein.

# Benefits of Keto Diet

Keto Diet can be beneficial in the following ways:

1. **It Controls your cravings:**

This can be possible when you control your general blood sugar levels helps you control your cravings. Several studies have revealed this to be truth.

2. **Keto Diet sharpens your brain:**

Keto Diet helps to sharpen the human brain and fuel it when glucose is absence. The brain also gets energies through the Keto diet.

3. **It helps to fall the Inflammation markers:**

Studies reveal that cases of inflammation come as a result of diverse health issues like diabetes, heart disease, and arthritis etc. The nutritional values of Ketosis have the capability to reduce inflammation.

4. **You are safe from type 2 diabetes:**

A study reveals that Keto Diet can improve blood sugar control for people living with type 2 diabetes. Being on Ketosis can drastically reduce your daily carbohydrates to less than 20g. This helps to manage or control the condition of the type 2 diabetes.

5. **It gives the human body more energy:**

Keto Diet is equipped with the ability of proving energy to the body. For those who are new to Keto Diet may experience Keto flu during the first few days of being on Keto Diet. Some may have fatigue, headaches, and nausea. When this happens, it simply connotes that your body is setting up itself from the usual burning of glucose to burning of fat for energy. Your body will gain more energy when it is fully switched.

## How to Kick-Start Ketosis

The Keto Diet is all about setting up your body to start burning fat instead of glucose when energy is needed by the body.

The keto Diet comprises of low carb (carbohydrate), and high fat diets. The Keto Diet has become popular in most parts of the globe because people have now come to like it due to its numerous health benefits. Starting the Keto diet is very simple but some people do have some doubt in them asking themselves if the keto Diet can work in them as it works for others. Starting the Keto Diet also requires that you know what Keto Diet is so that kick start with ease. Kick starting Ketosis could include: cutting down carbohydrates intake, eating high-quality fats, doing much exercise, maintaining your protein level.

# Meaning of Carbs

One of the ways in which the body obtains calories is through carbohydrates being are macronutrients. Carbs is a short form of saying carbohydrate while calories also mean energy. Carbohydrates according to several studies show that carbohydrate is the main source of energy. Carbohydrate is a combination of carbon, hydrogen and oxygen. That is why they are called carbohydrate. Normally, the daily consumption of 1g of carbohydrate is equivalent to 4 calories. This means a diet of 1,800 calories per day will give about 202g and 292g for both low and high end.

## Foods That Are High On Carbs

1. **Black Beans:** Beans are known to contain protein and fiber but they however contain traces of carbohydrates.

2. **Whole Wheat Pasta:** Whole wheat pasta contains a whole lot of carbs necessary for your body to get into Ketosis.

3. **Yogurt:** It may interest you to know that yogurt is high in carbohydrate. Yes sure, it is.

4. **Maple Syrup:** This is also a good source of carbohydrates despite the fact that they are sweetener, they also contains carbohydrates.

5. **Dates:** Their sizes are not necessary but they are a good source of carbohydrates.

6. **Corn:** Corn is stock with lots of carbohydrates which give more energy to the body for a healthy living.

7. **Quinoa:** They have traces of carbohydrates in their nutritional content. It's a good source of carbohydrate.

8. **Adzuki Beans:** These Asian beans. It origin come from China according to research. It is also a good source of carbohydrates.

9. **Chickpeas:** Chickpeas are high in carbohydrates. They are the main ingredient in hummus. They contain high level of carbohydrates.

10. **Grapefruit:** This citrus contains a good amount of carbohydrates.

11. **Oats:** Oats are good example of food that is high in carbohydrates. Many people begin their morning with oats.

12. **Sweet Potatoes:** Sweet potatoes are another source of carbohydrate. Although sweet potatoes contains lower carbs compared to the white potatoes.

# Foods to Eat on Keto Diet

1. **Beef:** Roast, Steak, veal, ground beef and stews.

2. **Poultry:** Quail, duck, Chicken breasts, turkey and wild game.

3. **Pork:** Tenderloin, Pork loin, chops, ham, and sugar-free bacon.

4. **Fish:** Tuna, salmon, Mackerel trout, halibut, cod, catfish, and mahi-mahi.

5. **Shellfish:** Clams, crab, Oysters, mussels, and lobster.

6. **Organ meats:** Liver, tongue, Heart, kidney, and offal.

7. **Eggs:** Fried, deviled, scrambled and boiled.

8. **Leafy greens:** Spinach, Kale, Swiss chard and arugula.

9. **Cruciferous vegetables:** Cauliflower, Cabbage, and zucchini.

10. **Lettuces:** Romaine, Iceberg, and butter-head.

11. **Oil:** Coconut butter, Coconut oil, Flaxseed oil, Olive oil, Sesame seed oil, MCT oil, Walnut oil, avocado oil, Heavy cream and heavy whipping cream.

# Foods To Avoid on Keto Diet

1. **Grains:** These are good sources of carbohydrates. When you are on Keto Diet, the best thing to do is to avoid foods that are grains. These include wheat; pasta, whole grains, rice, quinoa, oats, barley, rye, and corn.

2. **Sugar:** Avoid eating sugary things like artificial smoothies, sweeteners, soda, and fruit juice, ketchup and BBQ. They are all sauces of sugar, so avoid them.

3. **Alcohol:** The major content of alcohol is ethanol. This can stop your body from producing ketones. So avoid intake of alcohol. Some beverages contain alcohol.

4. **Starchy Veggies:** When you are on Keto Diet, try to avoid starchy vegetables for examples sweet potatoes, some squash, potatoes, parsnips, and carrots. Instead you may choose to like taking fruits as they are more beneficial in Keto Diets.

5. **Seed Oils:** When you heat seed oils in a skillet, they can become oxidized. You need to completely do away with canola oil, corn oil, and peanut oil. They are good source of omega 6 fatty acids. The acid could be inflammatory when they are in large amounts.

6. **Beans and Legumes:** Beans and legumes are very high in carbohydrate. You need to avoid consuming food like chickpeas, black beans, lentils and kidney beans.

# Smart Tips to Achieve Success On Keto Diet

1. **Make Use of Exogenous Ketones:**

This also helps to stick to Keto Diet because it is equivalent to MCT oil. Taking exogenous ketones is just a short way to get into ketosis.

2. **Count Your Carbohydrates:**

It is pertinent to adapt to a system of counting or measuring your daily intake of carbohydrate. You have to be very mindful because there are some hidden carbohydrates in some foods which may look Keto friendly but absolutely contain sugar. Such foods include the following: Milk, Chicken wings loaded with barbecue, blueberries, yogurt, breaded meats etc.

3. **Improve your Gut Micro-biome:**

Every human system is linked to gut health. Human gut micro-biome affects everything ranging from the mental health to the digestive system and many other systems found in the human body. When your gut flora is healthy, the metabolic flexibility, hormones, and insulin sensitivity in the body become more efficient and effective. When the body need to utilized energy, the above process can have an effect in your ability to change from carbohydrates to fats for energy. This help to achieve success on Keto Diet.

4. **Clear Out Your Kitchen:**

It is very important to make sure your kitchen is properly clean after every meal you prepare. This will make you convenient and prepare healthy meal. When your kitchen is clean, you will be highly compelled to stick to the Keto Diet. Replacing all of your carbs, except for non-starchy vegetables, with keto-friendly foods will help you stick to Keto Diet.

5. **Always Have Convenient Snacks On Hand:**

Concentrating on the Keto Diet needs time. Some people gets discouraged because of the lots of foods you need to prepare. In the absence of enough time, the alternative is to make lots of keto-friendly or carb heavy snacks when you have limited time. Such snacks include: Hard boiled eggs, Beef jerky, premade guacamole.

# Smart Tips for Eating Out on Keto Diet

New people on Keto Diet may find it difficult to identify foods that are Keto friendly and foods that are not Keto friendly. It is important to identify and know those Keto friendly foods while you are eating out. You do not need to eat anything you see out there. Most of the restaurants you will visit have a whole lot of Keto friendly foods which will prompt you to make your choice. Below are guidelines on how to stick to Keto Diet when you eat outside in the restaurant:

1. **Breakfast:**

If you are eating your breakfast in a restaurant, choose eggs and bacon and green salad on the sides regularly. This can substitute pancakes or toast.

2. **Lunch:**

Lunch is always alternatives to salad in some big restaurants. You can always replace the sugar filled dressings with vinegar or olive oil.

3. **Dinner:**

Almost all the restaurant will have meat-filled food. If you are eating your dinner in a restaurant, try to demand for their fattiest cut of steak like rib eye. You can as well replace the potatoes with vegetables. These tips help you stick to Keto Diet.

# SMOOTHIE & BREAKFAST RECIPES

## Green Smoothie

Preparation time: 5 minutes

Cooking time: 5 minutes

Overall time: 10 minutes

Serves: 2 to 4 people

**Recipe Ingredients:**

- 2/3 cup (20g) of spinach blend
- ½ of medium avocado (135g)
- 1 scoop (10g) of medium chain triglyceride(MCT) oil powder
- 1 teaspoon of pure vanilla extract
- ½ teaspoon of matcha powder
- 1 tablespoon (12g) of golden monk fruit sweetener
- 2/3 cup of water
- 5 ice cubes

**Optional additions:**

- ½ tablespoon (6g) of chia seeds, soaked in 2 tablespoon water for 15 minutes
- 1 tablespoon (6g) of collagen powder
- ¼ cup of vanilla protein powder
- ½ teaspoon maca root powder
- ½ teaspoon of turmeric

**Cooking Instructions:**

1. Add all ingredients to blender and blend until well-combined.
2. Serve immediately and enjoy!

Chocolate Fat Bomb Smoothie

Preparation time: 5 minutes

Cooking time: 5 minutes

Gross time: 10 minutes

Serves: 1 to 3 people

**Recipe Ingredients:**

- 2 ice cubes
- ½ cup (120ml) of unsweetened coconut milk (from a carton)
- ¼ cup (60g) of full-fat canned coconut cream
- 2 tablespoon (24g) of classic monk fruit sweetener
- 1 scoop (10g) (MCT) oil powder
- 1 tablespoon (16g) of no-sugar-added sun butter
- 1 tablespoon (5g) of unsweetened cocoa powder
- 1/16 teaspoon of salt

**Cooking Instructions:**

1. Add all ingredients and pulse until smooth to a high-speed blender.

2. Serve immediately and enjoy!

Breakfast Pizza

Preparation time: 10 minutes

Cooking time: 15 minutes

Gross time: 25 minutes

Serves: 2 to 4 people

**Recipe Ingredients:**

- 2 cups of grated cauliflower
- 2 tbsp. of coconut flour
- ½ tsp. of salt
- 4 eggs
- 1 tbsp. of psyllium husk powder

**Toppings:**

- Smoked salmon
- Avocado
- Herbs
- Spinach
- Olive oil

**Cooking Instructions:**

1. Preheat the oven to 350°F and line a pizza tray or sheet pan with parchment.

2. Add all ingredients in a mixing bowl, except toppings and mix until combined and set it aside for about 5 minutes.

3. Allow coconut flour and psyllium husk to absorb liquid and thicken up. Carefully pour the breakfast pizza base onto the pan.

4. Use your hands to mold it into a round, even pizza crust. Bake for about 15 minutes, or until golden brown and fully cooked.

5. Remove from the oven and top breakfast pizza with your chosen toppings. Serve warm and Enjoy!

## Golden Smoothie

Preparation time: 5 minutes

Cooking time: 5 minutes

Gross time: 10 minutes

Serve: 2 to 4 people

**Recipe Ingredients:**

- ¼ cup (60g) of canned coconut cream
- 1 scoop (10g) of MCT oil powder
- 1 tablespoon (7g) of freshly grated ginger
- 1 tablespoon (12g) of golden monk fruit sweetener
- ¾ teaspoon of ground turmeric
- ½ teaspoon of pure vanilla extract
- ⅛ teaspoon of black pepper
- ⅛ teaspoon of cinnamon
- 4 ice cubes
- ¼ cup + 2 tablespoons (3 ounces) cup of water, divided

**Cooking Instructions:**

1. Add all ingredients excluding water to a high speed blender.

2. After all ingredients are added to the blender and before turning blender on, pour in ¼ cup (2 ounces) of water and pulse until it is well-combined.

3. Remove blender lid, pour in remaining 2 tablespoons (1 ounces) of water, and blend again.

4. Serve immediately and Enjoy!

## Iced Matcha Latte

Preparation time: 5 minutes

Cooking time: 5 minutes

Overall time: 10 minutes

Serves: 1 to 3 people

**Recipe Ingredients:**

- 1 tsp. of high quality matcha powder
- ½ tbsp. of brain octane oil
- ½ tsp. of stevia powder
- 1 tsp. of vanilla
- 1 tbsp. of collagen protein
- 150g (or 1 cup) of coconut milk, frozen into ice cubes
- 1 cup of water
- 1/2 to 1 teaspoon of ashwagandha

**Cooking Instructions:**

1. Add all ingredients except collagen powder to a high-powered blender.

2. Blitz until it is well-combined and completely smooth. Taste and adjust the sweetness if needed.

3. Add the collagen lightly blend until just incorporated to avoid damaging proteins.

4. Pour over ice and enjoy immediately.

Mocha Smoothie

Preparation time: 5 minutes

Cooking time: 5 minutes

Gross time: 10 minutes

Serves: 1 to 3 people

**Recipe Ingredients:**

- ¼ cup + 2 tablespoons (90 mL) of heavy whipping cream
- ¼ cup (2 ounces) of water
- 2 tablespoon (24g) of classic monk fruit sweetener
- 2 teaspoons (3.3g) of unsweetened cocoa powder
- 1 ¼ teaspoons (2.5g) of espresso powder
- 1/16 teaspoon of salt
- 4 ice cubes

**Optional:**

- 1 scoop (10g) of MCT oil powder

**Cooking Instructions:**

1. To a high-speed blender, add all ingredients and pulse until just combined.

2. Be careful to not over-blend, which will lead to the smoothie being too thin.

3. Serve immediately and Enjoy!

## CBD Rooibos Tea Latte

Preparation time: 5 minutes

Cooking time: 5 minutes

Overall time: 10 minutes

Serves: 1 to 3 people

**Recipe Ingredients:**

- 1 cup of water
- 2 bags of rooibos tea
- 1 tbsp. of grass-fed butter or ghee
- 1 tsp. of Brain octane oil
- 1 scoop of collagen peptides
- 1 dropper full of CBD oil (about 10 mg, optional)

**Optional:**

- Liquid monk fruit extract to taste, ground Ceylon cinnamon

**Cooking Instructions:**

1. Boil water, add to a mug with both tea bags, and steep for about 5 minutes.
2. Remove tea bags and add in remaining ingredients except collagen. Pour mixture into a blender and blend until incorporated.
3. Add collagen and blend on the lowest speed until just incorporated to avoid damaging delicate proteins.
4. Enjoy hot, or pour over ice.

## Milkshake Smoothie with Raspberries

Preparation time: 5 minutes

Cooking time: 5 minutes

Overall time: 10 minutes

Serves: 2 to 4 people

**Recipe Ingredients:**

- 1 cup of unsweetened plain almond milk
- 1 cup of crushed ice
- ¼ cup of heavy whipping cream
- ¼ cup of fresh raspberries
- 2 tablespoons of confectioners swerve
- 1 tablespoons of cream cheese
- ½ teaspoon of vanilla extract
- Pinch of salt (<1/8 teaspoon)

**Cooking Instructions:**

1. Microwave cream cheese in a small bowl for about 5 seconds or until soft, add all ingredients to a blender. Blend until very smooth.

2. Taste and adjust accordingly by adding more Swerve for a sweeter taste, or another tablespoon of cream cheese for a creamier finish.

3. If using a different sweetener, add it to taste. Serve immediately. If not served right away, keep chilled in an ice bath.

4. Separation is normal so give it a stir before drinking.

Flu Smoothie

Preparation time: 5 minutes

Cooking time: 5 minutes

Gross time: 10 minutes

Serves: 2 to 4 people

**Recipe Ingredients**

- ½ cup of kale
- 2 large strawberries
- 50 grams of avocado
- ½ cup of cucumber, with peel
- ½ cup of unsweetened almond milk
- 1 tsp. of stevia
- 1 tsp. of vanilla extract
- ½ teaspoon of pink Himalayan salt

**Cooking Instructions:**

1. Add all ingredients to a blender. Blend until smooth. Chill or pour over ice.

2. Serve immediately and Enjoy!

Breakfast Egg Crepes

Preparation time: 5 minutes

Cooking time: 10 minutes

Overall time: 15 minutes

Servings: 1 to 3 people

**Recipe Ingredients:**

- 1 tsp. of olive oil
- 2 eggs
- Handful alfalfa sprouts
- ¼ avocado thinly sliced
- Few slices turkey cold cuts shredded
- 1 tsp. of mayonnaise

**Cooking Instructions:**

1. Heat oil in a small-medium sized pan over medium heat, once pan is hot crack the eggs into the pan.

2. Using your spatula lightly spread them around so they are the same thickness all around and completely covering the pan and cook until it is crispy.

3. Flip over and continue to cook for another minute.

4. Remove from pan, top with remaining ingredients in the center of the egg crepe and roll up tightly.

## Coffee Smoothie

Preparation time: 2 minutes

Cooking time: 2 minutes

Gross time: 4 minutes

Serves: 1 to 3 people

**Recipe Ingredients:**

- 4 ounces of coffee frozen into ice cubes
- 1.5 cups of unsweetened vanilla almond milk
- 1 tablespoon of perfect Keto MCT Oil
- 1 tablespoon of chia seeds
- 2 tablespoon of heavy whipping cream
- 1 teaspoon of vanilla extract
- 1/8 teaspoon of stevia

**Cooking Instructions:**

1. Freeze coffee in an ice cube tray, (12 ounces of coffee will fill a standard ice cube tray).

2. Add all ingredients to a blender and blend until smooth. Pour in a glass, serve immediately and enjoy!

Frosted Vanilla Blackberry Lemonade

Preparation time: 5 minutes

Cooking time: 5 minutes

Gross time: 10 minutes

Serves: 1 to 3 people

**Recipe Ingredients:**

- 2/3 cup of unsweetened almond
- ¼ cup of lemon juice
- 1 tablespoon of collagen
- 2 pinches of Himalayan salt or Mineral Salt
- 1 tsp. of vanilla extract
- ½ tsp. glucomannan
- ½ cup of blackberries, fresh or frozen
- 3 cups of ice cubes (around one full tray)

**Cooking Instructions:**

1. Put lemon juice, almond milk, collagen, stevia, salt, and vanilla in blender. Turn on low for just a few seconds to mix.

2. While blender is on low, slowly add in glucomannan. Blend on low for about 30 seconds and turn off.

3. Add in blackberries and ice cubes, blend on high until completely blended.

Chocolate Peanut Butter Smoothie

Preparation time: 5 minutes

Cooking time: 5 minutes

Gross time: 10 minutes

Serves: 1 to 3 people

**Recipe Ingredients:**

- ¼ cup Peanut butter (creamy)
- 3 tablespoons of cocoa powder
- 1 cup of heavy cream (or coconut cream for dairy-free or vegan)
- 1 ½ cup of unsweetened almond milk (regular or vanilla)
- 6 tablespoons of powdered erythritol (to taste)
- 1/8 teaspoon of sea salt (optional)

**Cooking Instructions:**

1. Combine all ingredients in a blender. Puree until it is smooth. Adjust sweetener to taste if desired.

2. Serve immediately and Enjoy!

## Salted Caramel Smoothie

Preparation time: 2 minutes

Cooking time: 2 minutes

Gross time: 4 minutes

Servings: 1 to 3 people

**Recipe Ingredients:**

- 1 bag of salted caramel tea steeped in 6 ounces of water
- 1 cup unsweetened almond milk
- 2 tablespoons of whipping cream
- 1 tablespoon of MCT oil
- ½ teaspoon of stevia
- ¾ teaspoon of xanthan gum
- 8 ice cubes

**Cooking Instructions:**

1. Steep 1 bag of Bigelow Salted Caramel Tea in 6 oz. water and remove and discard tea bag when done.

2. Combine remaining ingredients in a blender and blend until smooth. Pour into a glass and serve.

Coconut Milk Strawberry Smoothie

Preparation time: 2 minutes

Cooking time: 2 minutes

Gross time: 4 minutes

Serves: 1 to 3 people

**Recipe Ingredients:**

- 1 cup of strawberries frozen
- 1 cup of unsweetened coconut milk
- 2 tbsp. of smooth almond butter
- 2 packets of stevia optional

**Cooking Instructions:**

1. Add all ingredients to a blender. Blend until it is smooth.

2. Pour into glass and enjoy!

## Buttery Coconut Flour Waffles

Preparation time: 10 minutes

Cooking time: 20 minutes

Gross time: 30 minutes

Serves: 2 to 4 people

**Recipe Ingredients:**

- 4 tablespoons of coconut flour
- 5 eggs separate whites from yolks
- 4 tablespoon of granulated stevia
- 1 teaspoon of baking powder
- 2 teaspoon of vanilla extract
- 3 tablespoon of milk full fat
- ½ cup of butter melted
- Coconut flour waffles

**Cooking Instructions:**

1. In a bowl, mix the egg yolks, coconut flour, stevia, and baking powder. Add the melted butter slowly to the flour mixture.

2. Mix it well to ensure smooth consistency Add the milk and vanilla to the flour and butter mixture be sure to mix well.

3. In another bowl, whisk the egg whites until fluffy. Gently fold spoons of the whisked egg whites into the flour mixture.

4. Pour mixture into waffle maker and cook until golden brown. Serve immediately and Enjoy!

## Coconut Chia Smoothies

Preparation time: 5 minutes

Cooking time: 5 minutes

Gross time: 5 minutes

Serves: 2 to 4 people

**Recipe Ingredients:**

- 1 cup of frozen blueberries
- 1 cup of full fat Greek yogurt
- ½ cup of coconut cream
- 1 cup of unsweetened cashew or almond milk
- 2 tablespoons of coconut oil
- 2 tablespoons of ground chia seed
- 2 tablespoons of Swerve Sweetener or equivalent sweetener

**Cooking Instructions:**

1. Combine all ingredients in blender and blend until smooth.
2. Divide among 4 glasses. Serve immediately and Enjoy!

Fruit-Free Smoothie

Preparation time: 5 minutes

Cooking time: 5 minutes

Gross time: 5 minutes

Serves: 1 to 3 people

**Recipe Ingredients:**

- 1 cup of unsweetened almond milk
- ½ of avocado
- 2 cups of spinach
- ½ of scoop protein powder, I use Plant Fusion
- 1 teaspoon of cocoa powder
- 1 tablespoon of hemp seeds
- 1 tablespoon of MCT oil
- 10 drops of liquid stevia
- ½ cup of water for thinning out to desired consistency
- Ice cubes
- 1 teaspoon of cacao nibs (optional)

**Cooking Instructions:**

1. Add all the ingredients except cacao nibs to a blender and blend on high until smooth.

2. Pour into a glass and sprinkle with cacao nibs. Sip and Enjoy!

## Avocado Smoothie with Coconut Milk, Ginger, and Turmeric

Preparation time: 5 minutes

Cooking time: 10 minutes

Gross time: 15 minutes

Serves: 1 to 3 people

**Recipe Ingredients:**

- ½ avocado
- ¾ cup of full - fat coconut milk
- ¼ cup of almond milk
- 1 teaspoon of fresh grated ginger (about ½ inch piece)
- ½ teaspoon of turmeric
- 1 teaspoon of lemon or lime juice (or more to taste)
- 1 cup of crushed ice (or more for a thicker smoothie)
- Sugar-free sweetener to taste

**Cooking Instructions:**

1. Add the first 6 ingredients to a blender and blend on low-speed until smooth. Add crushed ice and sweetener.

2. Blend on high until it is smooth. Taste and adjust sweetness and tartness per your taste buds.

3. Adding a pinch of black pepper will make the curcumin in the turmeric more bioavailable and doesn't impact the taste.

4. Serve immediately and Enjoy!

## Blueberry Protein Power Smoothie

Preparation time: 2 minutes

Cooking time: 5 minutes

Overall time: 7 minutes

Serves: 1 to 3 people

**Recipe Ingredients:**

- ¼ cup of fresh blueberries
- 1 tablespoon of flaxseed meal
- 8 ounces of unsweetened almond milk
- 1 scoop of vanilla whey protein
- Low carb simple syrup optional
- 1 tablespoon of flaxseed meal
- 8 ounces of unsweetened almond milk
- 1 scoop of vanilla whey protein
- Low carb simple syrup optional

**Cooking Instructions:**

1. Mix all ingredients in a jug blender or immersion blender, and blend until smooth.

2. Test for sweetness and add syrup as desired. Serve immediately and Enjoy!

## Mocha Smoothie

Preparation time: 5 minutes

Cooking time: 5 minutes

Overall time: 5 minutes

Serves: 1 to 3 people

**Recipe Ingredients:**

- ½ cup of coconut milk
- 1 ½ cup of unsweetened almond milk
- 1 tsp. of vanilla extract
- 3 tbsp. of granulated stevia/erythritol blend
- 2 tsp. of instant coffee crystals regular of decaffeinated
- 3 tbsp. of unsweetened cocoa powder
- 1 avocado cut in half with pit removed

**Cooking Instructions:**

1. Place coconut milk, almond milk, vanilla extract, sweetener, coffee crystals, and cocoa powder into a blender.

2. Blend until smooth. Scoop the avocado into the mixture. Blend until smooth. Pour into glasses and serve.

Matcha Green Tea Smoothie

Preparation time: 2 minutes

Cooking time: 2 minutes

Gross time: 4 minutes

Serves: 1 to 3 people

**Recipe Ingredients:**

- ¾ cup of unsweetened almond milk or coconut milk
- 1 tbsp. of chia seeds
- 1 tsp. of matcha green tea powder
- ¼ tsp. of lemon juice
- 5 drops of vanilla stevia drops
- 2 tbsp. of plain whole milk Greek yogurt
- ¼ tsp. of glucomannon or xanthan gum
- ¼ cup of crushed ice optional

**Cooking Instructions:**

1. Combine all ingredients with blender until smooth. Sticky blender works best and is the easiest to clean.

2. Serve immediately and Enjoy!

## Fluffy Almond Flour Pancakes

Preparation time: 5 minutes

Cooking time: 5 minutes

Gross time: 10 minutes

Serves: 2 to 4 people

**Recipe Ingredients:**

- 1 ½ cups of blanched almond flour
- ½ teaspoon of baking soda
- 1 teaspoon of cinnamon (Ceylon preferred)
- ¼ teaspoon of sea salt
- 3 large pastured eggs, room temperature
- ¼ cup of pure coconut milk
- 1 tablespoon of unsalted butter (or coconut oil)
- 1/8 tsp. of liquid stevia
- 2 teaspoon of pure vanilla extract
- ¼ teaspoons of apple cider vinegar

**Cooking Instructions:**

1. Preheat griddle over medium heat. Place all of the liquid ingredients into your blender, then place all of the dry ingredients on top.

2. Cover and blend on low to start, then increase to high and blend at least 1 full minute.

3. Grease preheated griddle with butter (or coconut oil). Ladle a spoonful of batter onto the griddle to form a silver dollar size pancake.

4. Flip once the batter starts to bubble Repeat until you're done with the batter!

5. Serve immediately and Enjoy!

Mint Coco Smoothie

Preparation time: 5 minutes

Cooking time: 5 minutes

Overall time: 10 minutes

Serves: 2 to 4 people

**Recipe Ingredients:**

- 4 ounces of full fat coconut milk
- 4 ounces of water
- ½ cup of frozen cauliflower
- ½ avocado
- 1 scoop of collagen protein
- 1 teaspoon of vanilla extract
- 1 tablespoon of chopped mint
- 1 tablespoon of cacao powder
- 1 tablespoon of coconut oil
- Dash of Ceylon cinnamon
- Dash of Himalayan sea salt

**Optional toppings:**

- coconut flakes, chia seeds, flaxseeds, hemp seeds, pumpkin seeds, sliced macadamia nuts

**Cooking Instructions:**

1. Throw all ingredients into a blender and blend until very smooth and creamy.

2. Serve immediately and Enjoy!

## Cinnamon Chocolate Breakfast Smoothie

Preparation time: 5 minutes

Cooking time: 5 minutes

Gross time: 10 minutes

Serves: 1 to 3 people

**Recipe Ingredients:**

- ¾ cup coconut milk
- ½ ripe avocado
- 2 tsp. of unsweetened cacao powder
- 1 tsp. of cinnamon powder
- ¼ tsp. of vanilla extract
- Stevia to taste
- ½ tsp. of MCT oil or 1 teaspoon coconut oil (optional)

**Cooking Instructions:**

1. Blend all the ingredients together well.
2. Serve immediately and Enjoy!

# BRUNCH & DINNER RECIPES

## French Toast Sticks

Preparation time: 5 minutes

Cooking time: 10 minutes

Overall time: 15 minutes

**Recipe Ingredients:**

- 3 slices of Low Carb Bread
- 2 large eggs
- ¼ heavy cream
- 1 teaspoon of cinnamon
- ¼ cup of granulated sweetener
- 3 tablespoon of butter

**Cooking Instructions:**

1. Cut bread into sticks, whisk eggs, cream and cinnamon. Soak bread into egg mixture.

2. Heat skillet to medium high, melt butter (carefully not to brown) Pan fry French toast sticks until golden on each side.

3. Mix cinnamon and sweetener. Coat French toast sticks. Dip in sugar free syrup.

4. Serve immediately and Enjoy!

## Raspberry Cheesecake Bars

Preparation time: 5 minutes

Cooking time: 5 minute

Overall time: 10 minutes

Serves: 1 to 3 people

**Recipe Ingredients**

**For the macaroon crust:**

- ½ cup of butter, softened
- ½ cup of granulated sugar substitute
- ½ cup of desiccated unsweetened coconut
- ¼ cup of coconut flour
- ½ teaspoon of baking powder

**For the filling:**

- 8 ounces of cream cheese, softened
- 1/3 cup of granulated sugar substitute
- ¾ teaspoon of vanilla extract
- 1 egg
- 1 cup of raspberries
- 2 tablespoons of granulated sugar substitute

**Cooking Instructions:**

1. Cream together the butter and sugar substitute. Add the coconut, coconut flour and baking powder, mixing until thoroughly combined.

2. Press into a lightly greased 9 x 9 pan and set it aside. Beat the cream cheese and sugar substitute together until smooth.

3. Add the egg and vanilla extract and mix until thoroughly combined. Pour mixture over the crust.

4. Mash the raspberries and sugar substitute together in a small bowl with a fork. Drop by spoonful over the cheesecake mixture.

5. Then swirl it gently with the fork until distributed over the entire top, don't over mix. Bake in a 350°F oven for about 25 minutes. Remove and chill before serving.

Chia Jam

Preparation time: 5 minutes

Cooking time: 10 minutes

Overall time: 15 minutes

Serves: 8 to 12 people

**Recipe Ingredients:**

- 2 cups of berries of choice fresh or frozen
- 1 tbsp. of lemon juice freshly squeezed
- 2 tbsp. of chia seeds or more as needed
- 3 tbsp. of swerve or sweetener of choice, to taste

**Cooking Instructions:**

1. Cook your berries of choice in a saucepan over medium heat until they begin to break down, for about 5 minutes.

2. Stir in the lemon juice and sweetener of choice. Mash it down or leave it chunky. Cook for 5 more minutes, remove from heat and stir in the chia seeds.

3. Let stand until it begins to thicken, adding water if needed to thin out until desired consistency is reached.

4. Allow to cool to room temperature and store in an airtight container in the fridge for a week or two and in the freezer for up to three.

5. Serve immediately and Enjoy!

## Raspberry Linzer Cookie Bars

Preparation time: 5 minutes

Cooking time: 5 minutes

Overall time: 10 minutes

Serves: 2 to 4 people

**Recipe Ingredients:**

**For the crust:**

- 6 tbsp. of butter melted
- 2 cups of almond flour
- ½ cup of granulated sweetener
- ½ tsp. of vanilla extract

**For the filling:**

- ½ cup of sugar free with fiber raspberry preserves
- ¼ tsp. of xanthan gum
- 1/8 tsp. of almond extract

**Cooking Instructions:**

1. Combine the melted butter, almond flour, sweetener, and vanilla extract in a medium bowl and stir well until a stiff dough forms.

2. Line an 8 x 8 baking pan with parchment paper and press 2/3 of the crust dough into the bottom.

3. In a small bowl combine the jelly, xanthan gum, and almond extract and stir well. Spread the jelly mixture evenly over the crust.

4. Crumble the remaining crust mixture over the top of the jelly layer. Bake in a preheated oven at 350°F for about 30 minutes or until golden brown and firm.

5. Remove from the oven and cool completely before cutting into 2 inch squares. Serve immediately and Enjoy!

## Lemon Poppy Seed Donuts

Preparation time: 15 minutes

Cooking time: 15 minutes

Overall time: 30 minutes

Serves: 6 to 8 people

**Recipe Ingredients:**

**Donuts:**

- ½ cup of coconut flour
- ¼ cup of swerve sweetener
- 1 tablespoons of poppy seeds
- 1 teaspoon of baking powder
- ¼ teaspoon of salt
- 4 large eggs
- ¼ cup of ghee melted
- 2 teaspoons of lemon zest
- 7 tablespoons of water
- ½ teaspoons of lemon extract

**Glaze:**

- ¼ cup of powdered Swerve Sweetener
- 2 tablespoon of fresh lemon juice

**Cooking Instructions:**

1. Preheat the oven to 350°F and grease a donut pan very well. Whisk together the coconut flour, sweetener, poppy seed, baking powder, and salt in a medium bowl.

2. Stir in the eggs, ghee, lemon zest, 6 tablespoons of water, and lemon extract until it is well combined. Add additional water if the batter is very thick.

3. Divide the batter among the wells of the donut pan. If you have a six-well donut pan, you may need to work in batches.

4. Bake for about 15 minutes, until the donuts are set and firm to the touch. Remove and let cool in the pan for about 10 minutes.

5. Flip out onto a wire rack to cool completely. In a small bowl, whisk together the powdered sweetener and enough lemon juice to achieve a drizzling consistency.

6. Drizzle over the cooled donuts and serve.

## Blueberry Jam

Preparation time: 1 minute

Cooking time: 20 minutes

Overall time: 21 minutes

Serves: 10 to 14 people

**Recipe Ingredients:**

- 2 cups / 300g of blueberries, frozen or fresh
- 2 tablespoons of water
- juice of ½ lemon
- 2 pinches of xanthan gum

**Optional:**

- 1 tsp. vanilla extract

**Cooking Instructions:**

1. Put the blueberries, water and lemon juice (and vanilla, if using) in a nonstick pan, cover and allow to boil.

2. Remove the lid and cook on a medium heat for about 15 minutes, stirring regularly. The mixture will reduce by 1/3 and thicken.

3. Smash the berries with a spoon while they cook. You can blend the mixture if you wish to have a smooth consistency.

4. At the end, take a couple of pinches xanthan gum and sprinkle it evenly into the pot, stirring well afterwards.

5. Xanthan gum is a brilliant thickening agent and is also used in gluten free baking, so it does come in handy.

6. Pour the mixture into a clean jar and store in the fridge. This recipe fills a small (200ml) jar.

7. Serve immediately and Enjoy!

## Cappuccino Muffins

Preparation time: 20 minutes

Cooking time: 25 minutes

Gross time: 45 minutes

Serves: 8 to 12 people

**Recipe Ingredients:**

**Muffins:**

- ½ cup of sour cream
- 4 large eggs
- 1 teaspoon of espresso powder
- ½ teaspoon of vanilla extract
- 2 cups of almond flour
- ½ cup of swerve sweetener
- ¼ cup of coconut flour
- 2 teaspoon of baking powder
- 1 teaspoon cinnamon
- ¼ teaspoon of salt

**Glaze:**

- ¼ cup of powdered swerve sweetener
- 2 tablespoons of heavy whipping cream
- Cinnamon for garnish

**Cooking Instructions:**

1. Preheat oven to 350°F and line a muffin tin with parchment or silicone liners.

2. Combine sour cream, eggs, espresso powder, and vanilla extract in a large blender jar.

3. Blend for about 30 seconds. Add the almond flour, sweetener, coconut flour, baking powder, cinnamon, and salt.

4. Blend again until smooth, for about 30 seconds to a minute. If your batter is overly thick, add ¼ to ½ cup of water to thin it out.

5. Divide the mixture among the prepared muffin cups and bake for about 25 minutes, until just golden brown and firm to the touch.

6. Remove and let cool completely. In a small bowl, whisk together the powdered sweetener and cream. Drizzle over the cooled muffins.

7. Sprinkle with a little cinnamon and serve.

## Strawberry Scones

Preparation time: 5 minutes

Cooking time: 5 minutes

Overall time: 10 minutes

Serves: 6 to 8 people

**Recipe Ingredients:**

- 2 ¼ cups of blanched almond flour
- ¼ cup of coconut flour
- 2 tsp. of aluminum-free baking powder
- ½ tsp. of Himalayan salt
- ½ cup of non-GMO erythritol
- ½ tsp. of stevia
- 2 eggs
- ½ cup of coconut oil, melted
- 1 tsp. of vanilla extract
- 1 cup of chopped strawberries, fresh or frozen. If using frozen, thaw slightly to chop

**Cooking Instructions:**

1. Preheat oven to 350°F and line a large baking pan with parchment paper.

2. Whisk the almond flour, coconut flour, baking powder, salt, and sweetener together in a large bowl.

3. In a small bowl whisk the eggs, coconut oil, and vanilla. Add to the dry ingredients and mix thoroughly and add in strawberries.

4. Divide the dough into eight large clumps on the baking pan several inches apart. Pat the dough into triangles or circles about 3/4" inch tall.

5. Bake for about 22 to 25 minutes, until golden brown. Let it set in pan for about 5 to 10 minutes then remove to a wire rack to cool or eat while warm.

6. Serve immediately and Enjoy!

## Pistachio Shortbread Cookies

Preparation time: 5 minutes

Cooking time: 5 minutes

Overall time: 10 minutes

Serves: 2 to 4 people

**Recipe Ingredients:**

- 6 tablespoon of butter, melted
- 2 cups of superfine almond flour
- ½ cup of confectioner's style erythritol sweetener
- ½ cup of chopped pistachios
- 1 teaspoon of vanilla extract

**Cooking Instructions:**

1. Combine all of the cookie ingredients in a medium bowl and mix well. Form into a long roll and wrap tightly with plastic wrap.

2. Chill for about 30 minutes. Unwrap and slice into ½ inch thick rounds. Bake at 350°F for 12 minutes or until golden brown at the edges.

3. Serve immediately and Enjoy!

## Cherry Clafoutis

Preparation time: 5 minutes

Cooking time: 5 minutes

Overall time: 10 minutes

Serves: 8 to 12 people

**Recipe Ingredients:**

- 1 tablespoon of salted butter
- 1 cup of unsweetened almond milk
- 1/4 cup of heavy whipping cream
- 1/3 cup of granulated sugar substitute (I used this brand)
- 1/2 teaspoon of cherry extract (I used this brand)
- 1 tablespoon of vanilla extract
- ½ teaspoon of xanthan gum
- Pinch of kosher salt
- 6 eggs
- 1 cup of almond flour (I used this brand)
- 1.5 cups of fresh cherries, pitted and halved

**Cooking Instructions:**

1. Preheat oven to 400°F and use the butter to grease a 9 or 10" cast iron pan or baking dish.

2. Combine the almond milk, heavy cream, sweetener, cherry extract, vanilla extract, xanthan gum, salt, and eggs in a blender and blend for about 10 seconds.

3. Add the almond flour and blend for an additional 30 seconds or until smooth. Pour the mixture into the pan or muffin tins.

4. Spread the cherries, cut side up evenly over the top of the batter. Bake for about 18 to 20 minutes if making 4" muffins.

5. Bake for about 35 minutes if making in one large pan and serve warm or chilled.

## Blueberry Pancake Bites

Preparation time: 15 minutes

Cooking time: 25 minutes

Gross time: 40 minutes

Serves: 10 to 12 people

**Recipe Ingredients:**

- 4 large eggs
- ¼ cup of swerve sweetener
- ½ teaspoon of vanilla extract
- ½ cup of coconut flour
- ¼ cup butter melted
- 1 teaspoon of baking powder
- ½ teaspoon of salt
- ¼ teaspoon of cinnamon
- ½ cup of water
- ½ cup of frozen wild blueberries

**Cooking Instructions:**

1. Preheat oven to 325ºF and grease a mini muffin tin (24 cavity) very well. In a blender combine the eggs, sweetener and vanilla extract.

2. Blend until it is smooth. Add the coconut flour, melted butter, baking powder, salt, and cinnamon.

3. Blend again until smooth. It will seem very liquid but let it sit a few minutes and it will thicken up considerably.

4. Add 1/3 cup of the water and blend again. If it's still very thick, add a little additional water.

5. You shouldn't be able to pour it, but you should be able to scoop it out of the blender easily. Divide among the prepared muffin cups.

6. Add a few blueberries to each just about right. Press them gently into the batter. Bake for about 20 to 25 minutes, until it is set.

7. Let cool a few minutes in the pan and then serve with your favorite low carb pancake syrup.

8. Serve immediately and Enjoy!

## Almond Crescent Cookies

Preparation time: 5 minutes

Cooking time: 5 minutes

Gross time: 10 minutes

Serves: 2 to 4 people

**Recipe Ingredients:**

- 1 stick of salted butter, softened (1/2 cup)
- Pinch of kosher salt
- ½ cup of granulated erythritol sweetener
- ½ teaspoon of vanilla extract
- 1 teaspoon of almond extract
- 2 cups of superfine almond flour
- 1/3 cup of sliced almonds

**Cooking Instructions:**

1. Beat the butter, salt, and sweetener until fluffy. Add the vanilla and almond extracts and blend well.

2. Add the almond flour and beat until just blended to a stiff dough. Divide the dough into 12 balls. Roll each ball into a 3-inch log.

3. Spread the sliced almonds onto a clean surface and crush slightly into smaller pieces with the heel of your hand.

4. Roll the logs in the almond pieces and then bend the two ends in and pinch slightly to create a crescent shape.

5. Place the almond crescents on a parchment lined cookie sheet and bake in a preheated 350°F oven for about 15 minutes.

6. Remove and cool before serving.

## Cloud Bread Cheese Danish

Preparation time: 5 minutes

Cooking time: 30 minutes

Overall time: 35 minutes

Serves: 10 to 12 people

**Recipe Ingredients:**

**Cream Cheese Filling:**

- 8 oz. of cream cheese softened
- ½ tsp. of vanilla stevia drops for filling
- 1 egg yolk optional

**Base Egg Dough:**

- 4 eggs divided
- ¼ tsp. of vanilla stevia drops for dough
- 3 oz. of cream cheese softened
- ¼ cup of unflavored whey protein
- 1 tbsp. of coconut flour optional
- ½ tsp. of cream of tartar

**Cooking Instructions:**

1. Preheat oven to 325°F and line two baking sheets with parchment paper. In medium bowl, stir together 8 ounces of cream cheese and vanilla stevia.

2. Transfer to plastic bag or pastry bag. Separate egg whites and yolks into separate mixing bowls. Add stevia, 3 ounces of cream cheese and whey protein to yolks.

3. Stir in optional coconut flour, if using. Mix until smooth. Whip eggs whites with cream of tartar until stiff peaks form.

4. Gently fold yolk mixture into beaten whites. Spoon 6 mounds of the egg batter onto each prepared baking sheets.

5. Flatten each mound slightly. Pipe sweetened cream cheese onto the center of each batter circle. Bake at 325°F for about 30 minutes and serve.

## Pistachio Truffles Fat Bombs

Preparation time: 5 minutes

Cooking time: 5 minutes

Overall time: 10 minutes

Serves: 8 to 10 people

**Recipe Ingredients:**

- 8 oz. (1 cup) of mascarpone cheese, softened
- ¼ tsp. of pure vanilla extract
- 3 tbsp. of confectioners style erythritol sweetener
- ¼ cup of chopped pistachios

**Cooking Instructions:**

1. In a small bowl, combine the mascarpone, vanilla, and sweetener. Mix gently but thoroughly with a fork or spatula, until well blended and smooth.

2. Roll by hand into 10 balls, about 1 inch in diameter. Place the pistachios on a small plate and roll the truffles in them until completely coated.

3. Chill for about 30 minutes before serving. Store in an airtight container in the refrigerator for up to one week or in the freezer for up to 3 months.

## Avocado Egg

Preparation time: 5 minutes

Cooking time: 15 minutes

Overall time: 20 minutes

Serves: 2 to 4 people

**Recipe Ingredients:**

- 1 medium avocado
- 2 eggs
- 1-piece of bacon cooked and crumbled
- 1 tablespoon of low-fat cheese
- Pinch salt

**Cooking Instructions:**

1. Preheat oven to 425°F and begin by cutting the avocado in half and removing the pit.

2. Using a spoon, scoop out some of the avocado so it's a tad bigger than your egg and yolk.

3. Place in a muffin pan to keep the avocado stable while cooking. Crack your egg and add it to the inside of your avocado.

4. Sprinkle a little cheese on top with a pinch of salt. Top with cooked bacon. Cook for 14 to 16 minutes.

5. Serve warm and enjoy!

## Baked Denver Omelet

Preparation time: 5 minutes

Cooking time: 30 minutes

Gross time: 35 minutes

Serves: 6 people

**Recipe Ingredients:**

- ½ cup of chopped red bell pepper (chop veggies small)
- ½ cup of chopped green bell pepper
- 1/3 cup of chopped yellow onion
- 2 teaspoon of olive oil
- 1 cup (heaping) of chopped cooked ham
- 8 large eggs
- 1/3 cup of milk
- Salt and freshly ground black pepper
- ½ cup of shredded sharp cheddar cheese
- Sliced avocados, for serving (optional)
- Chopped chives and hot sauce, for serving (optional)

**Cooking Instructions:**

1. Preheat oven to 400°F. Spray a 7 by 11-inch or 9 by 9-inch baking dish with cooking spray. Sprinkle ham into an even layer in bottom of baking dish.

2. Heat oil in a skillet over medium-high heat. Once hot, add red and green bell peppers and onion and cook until softened, for about 4 minutes.

3. Evenly pour pepper mixture over ham layer then sprinkle evenly with cheese. In a large mixing bowl whisk together eggs and milk until well blended.

4. Season with salt and pepper and stir, then pour over mixture in baking dish. Bake in preheated oven until puffy and set, for about 22 to 25 minutes.

5. Cut and serve warm with avocado slices and optional chives and hot sauce.

# POULTRY RECIPES

### Golden Chicken Bacon Fritter Balls

Preparation time: 10 minutes

Cooking time: 30 minutes

Overall time: 40 minutes

Serves: 4 to 6 people

**Recipe Ingredients:**

- 1 chicken breast, minced
- 4 slices of bacon, diced
- 1 egg
- 2 green onions
- 2 cloves of garlic, peeled
- ¼ cup (60 ml) of olive oil
- ½ cup (60 g) of almond flour

**Cooking Instructions:**

1. Preheat oven to 350°F and line a baking tray with parchment paper. Process the chicken, bacon, egg, green onions, and garlic together.

2. Form 12 chicken bacon balls. Dip the balls into the olive oil then into the almond flour.

3. Place on the lined baking tray and bake for about 30 minutes until it turns golden on the outside.

4. Serve immediately and Enjoy!

## Chicken Tenders

Preparation time: 10 minutes

Cooking time: 20 minutes

Overall time: 30 minutes

Serves: 2 to 4 people

**Recipe Ingredients:**

- 3 chicken breasts
- 1 cup of coconut flour
- 3 tbsp. of curry powder
- 1 tbsp. of cumin powder
- 2 tsp. of turmeric powder
- 1 tbsp. of garlic powder
- Salt to taste

**Cooking Instructions:**

1. Preheat oven to 350F and cut the chicken breasts into approximately 1 by 3 inch strips. Mix the coconut flour with the spices in a bowl.

2. Add salt to taste. Drop each piece of chicken into the "breading" mixture and press the mixture onto the chicken strip so that it gets a thin covering.

3. Place on a baking tray and bake for about 20 minutes and serve.

Garlic Bacon Wrapped Chicken Bites

Preparation time: 10 minutes

Cooking time: 30 minutes

Gross time: 40 minutes

Serves: 1 to 3 people

**Recipe Ingredients:**

- 1 large chicken breast, cut into small bites
- 8–9 thin slices of bacon, cut into thirds
- 3 tbsp. of garlic powder (or 6 crushed garlic if preferred)

**Cooking Instructions:**

1. Preheat oven to 400°F and line a baking tray with aluminum foil. Place the garlic powder into a bowl and dip each chicken bite into the garlic powder.

2. Wrap each short bacon piece around each garlic chicken bite. Place the bacon wrapped chicken bites on the baking tray.

3. Try to space them out so they're not touching. Bake for 25 to 30 minutes until the bacon turns crispy. Turn the pieces after 15 minutes if you can remember.

4. Serve immediately and Enjoy!

## Chicken and Bacon Sausages

Preparation time: 10 minutes

Cooking time: 20 minutes

Overall time: 30 minutes

Serves: 10 to 12 people

**Recipe Ingredients:**

- 2 large chicken breasts, or use 1 lb. ground chicken
- 2 slices bacon, cooked and broken into small bits
- 1 egg, whisked
- 2 tbsp. of Italian seasoning
- 2 tsp. of garlic powder
- 2 tsp. of onion powder
- Salt and pepper

**Cooking Instructions:**

1. Preheat oven to 425°F and process all the ingredients together in a food processor.

2. Form 12 thin patties (1/2-inch thick) from the meat mixture and place on a baking tray lined with foil.

3. Bake for about 20 minutes. Check with a meat thermometer that the internal temperature of a patty near the middle of the tray is 170°F.

4. Cool and store in fridge or freezer, serve Enjoy!

## Chicken, Bacon, and Apple Mini Meatloaves

Preparation time: 15 minutes

Cooking time: 25 minutes

Overall time: 40 minutes

Serves: 2 to 4 people

**Recipe Ingredients:**

- 1 ½ apples, diced into small cubes
- 2 chicken breasts, minced
- 10 slices of bacon, cooked and crushed into bits
- 3 tbsp. of olive oil or avocado oil
- 1 tsp. of salt (more to taste)

**Cooking Instructions:**

1. Preheat oven to 400°F and process the chicken breast in food processor if it's not already minced. Cook the bacon, and dice the apple.

2. Mix all the ingredients together in a large bowl. Grease a muffin pan and fill with the meat mixture or use these non-stick silicone muffin pans.

3. Bake for about 20 to 25 minutes. Check with a meat thermometer that the internal temperature reaches 170°F.

4. Serve immediately and Enjoy!

## Crispy Baked Buffalo Wings

Preparation time: 15 minutes

Cooking time: 1 hour

Gross time: 1 hour 15 minutes

Serves: 2 to 4 people

**Recipe Ingredients:**

- 1 lb. of chicken wings
- 1 tsp. of sea salt
- ¼ tsp. of ground black pepper
- 3 tbsp. of virgin coconut oil
- 3 tbsp. of apple cider vinegar
- 3 tbsp. of fresh lemon juice
- ½ tsp. of cayenne
- ½ tsp. of paprika
- 1 tsp. of garlic powder
- 1 tsp. of onion powder

**Cooking Instructions:**

1. Preheat oven to 400°F and line a baking sheet with parchment paper. Wash and pat dry each chicken wing.

2. Dust evenly with ½ teaspoon of the sea salt plus the ground pepper. Bake at 400°F for approximately one hour, or until golden brown.

3. While the chicken is baking, make the buffalo sauce in a small sauce pan over the stove. Whisk the coconut oil, vinegar, lemon juice, cayenne, paprika, garlic powder, onion powder, and remaining 1 teaspoon of sea salt together.

4. Let it simmer for about 5 minutes then remove from heat. Whisk again just before using. When the chicken comes out of the oven.

5. Let them rest for about 5 minutes then place in a large bowl and pour the buffalo sauce over. Stir and combine until each wing is evenly coated.

6. Serve alongside celery sticks and homemade ranch.

## Tandoori Chicken Wings with Mint Chutney

Preparation time: 5 minutes

Cooking time: 5 minutes

Overall time: 10 minutes

Serves: 2 to 4 people

**Recipe Ingredients:**

- 18 whole chicken wings
- 1 tbsp. of ground ginger
- 1 tbsp. of ground cumin
- 1 tbsp. of ground coriander
- 1 tbsp. of paprika
- 1 tbsp. of turmeric
- 1 tbsp. of sea salt
- 1 tbsp. of cayenne pepper
- 2 tbsp. of olive oil
- Mint Chutney
- 1 cup of fresh mint
- ¾ cup of fresh cilantro (including stems)
- 1 1/2 -inch of piece fresh ginger
- ½ tbsp. of lime juice
- 1 tbsp. of olive oil
- 1 medium serrano pepper
- 1 tbsp. of water
- Sea salt (to taste)

**Cooking Instructions:**

1. In a large bowl mix together the Tandoori spice blend. Pat the wings dry and toss in the bowl with 2 tablespoons of olive oil.

2. Toss with the spices until every wing is covered. Cover bowl and place in refrigerator at least 20 minutes.

3. Preheat your grill to high. Grill wings for about 25 minutes flipping occasionally and rotating placement for even cooking.

4. While wings are grilling blend the ingredients for the chutney into a smooth sauce. Add a bit more water if needed.

5. Season with salt to fit your taste. Serve immediately and Enjoy!

## Grilled Cilantro Lime Chicken Wings

Preparation time: 5 minutes

Cooking time: 10 minutes

Gross time: 15 minutes

Serves: 2 to 4 people

**Recipe Ingredients:**

- 2 pounds of chicken wings (about 20)
- 1 handful of fresh cilantro
- 1 medium Lime (juiced)
- 1 medium Jalapeño
- 2 cloves of garlic
- 3 tbsp. of coconut oil
- 1 tsp. of sea salt
- Lime wedges for serving
- 1 batch of Jalapeño Ranch Dip

**Cooking Instructions:**

1. Blend together cilantro, lime juice, jalapeno, garlic, and coconut oil.

2. Toss the cilantro lime marinade with chicken. Marinate the chicken for at least 2 hours or overnight.

3. Heat your grill to high and grill wings for about 5 to 7 minutes per side, or until crisp and no longer pink in the middle.

4. Serve with a squeeze of lime and jalapeño ranch dip.

## Chicken Bulgogi with Sesame Garnish

Preparation time: 10 minutes

Cooking time: 15 minutes

Gross time: 25 minutes

Serves: 1 to 3 people

**Recipe Ingredients:**

- 3 tbsp. of avocado oil (45 ml), to cook with
- 1 chicken breast, cut into thin strips
- ½ medium onion, diced
- 3 tbsp. (45 ml) of gluten-free tamari sauce or coconut amino
- ½ tbsp. (7.5 ml) of sesame oil
- 2 cloves of garlic, minced or finely diced
- 1 tsp. (5 g) of sesame seeds (for garnish)
- Salt, to taste

**Cooking Instructions:**

1. Add avocado oil to a large skillet over medium-high heat.

2. Add the chicken and onion to the skillet and Sauté until the chicken is cooked through, for about 5 to 7 minutes.

3. Add the tamari sauce or coconut amino, sesame oil, and garlic to the skillet and Sauté for about 1 minute. Season with salt, to taste.

4. Garnish with sesame seeds. Serve immediately and Enjoy!

## Asian Chicken Thighs

Preparation time: 5 minutes

Cooking time: 6 hours

Gross time: 6 hours 5 minutes

Serves: 2 to 4 people

**Recipe Ingredients:**

- 8 chicken thighs (with skin on)
- ½ onion, sliced
- ½ cup (120 ml) of tamari sauce
- ¼ cup (60 ml) of water
- 4 cloves of garlic, minced
- Salt and pepper, to taste
- 1 green onion, chopped for garnish
- 1 tsp. (5 g) of sesame seeds, for garnish

**Cooking Instructions:**

1. Place the chicken thighs at the bottom of the pot. Then add in the sliced onions, tamari sauce, water, and garlic.

2. Try to cover most of the chicken in the sauce. Set on low heat for 6 hours. Season with salt and pepper, to taste.

3. Garnish with chopped green onions and sesame seeds. Roast the thighs in the oven on a baking tray for about 15 to 20 minutes to brown and crisp up the skin.

4. Serve immediately and Enjoy!

## Chicken Massaman Curry with Daikon Radishes

Preparation time: 15 minutes

Cooking time: 25 minutes

Gross time: 40 minutes

Serves: 2 to 4 people

**Recipe Ingredients:**

- 1/2 onion, diced
- 2 chicken breasts, diced
- 3 tbsp. (45 ml) of coconut oil, to cook with
- 2 cups (480 ml) of coconut milk
- 3 tbsp. of curry powder
- 1 tbsp. of ginger, minced
- 1 tbsp. (15 ml) of fish sauce
- 1/4 cup (60 ml) of almond butter
- 2 tbsp. (30 ml) of lime juice
- 1 Daikon radish (300 g) of peeled and diced
- 2 tbsp. of cilantro, chopped
- Salt and pepper, to taste

**Cooking Instructions:**

1. Add coconut oil to a large pan and brown the onions. Then, add the chicken and brown.

2. Add coconut milk, curry powder, ginger, fish sauce, almond butter, daikon radishes, and lime juice and simmer for about 15 minutes.

3. Add in cilantro and salt to taste. Serve immediately and Enjoy

## Caprese Hasselback Chicken

Preparation time: 10 minutes

Cooking time: 25 minutes

Overall time: 35 minutes

Serves: 2 to 4 people

**Recipe Ingredients:**

- 4 large chicken breasts, (6 ounces each)
- 4 ounces of fresh mozzarella cheese, the kind that comes in a log
- 2 medium roma tomatoes, sliced
- ¼ cup of fresh basil, divided (half of it cut into ribbons)
- 2 tablespoons of olive oil
- 2 tablespoons of balsamic vinegar
- Sea salt & pepper

**Cooking Instructions:**

1. Preheat the oven to 400°F and line a baking sheet with parchment paper or foil. Make 5 to 6 deep slits in each chicken breast, and do not cut the way through.

2. Season both sides with sea salt and black pepper. Place onto the lined baking sheet. Slice the tomatoes and mozzarella very thinly, about 1/8" to ¼ " thick.

3. Cut the pieces to a width wider than the thickness of your chicken breast. Stuff a piece of mozzarella, a tomato slice, and a basil leaf into each slit in the chicken.

4. Drizzle olive oil and balsamic vinegar over the chicken. Bake for about 20 to 25 minutes, until cooked through (heated to 160°F with a meat thermometer).

5. When the chicken is ready, sprinkle remaining fresh basil ribbons on top right before serving. If desired, drizzle with additional balsamic vinegar.

## Chicken Korma

Preparation time: 8 minutes

Cooking time: 25 minutes

Overall time: 33 minutes

Serves: 3 to 5 people

**Recipe Ingredients:**

- ¼ cup of almond butter
- 3 cloves of garlic peeled
- 1 ½ inch piece of fresh ginger root, peeled and chopped
- 2 ½ tbsp. of ghee or butter
- ½ medium sized onion minced
- 1 tsp. of ground coriander
- 1 tsp. of garam masala
- 1 tsp. of ground cumin
- 1 tsp. of ground turmeric
- 1 tsp. of chili powder
- 3 skinless boneless chicken breast halves - diced
- 1/3 cup of tomato sauce
- 1/3 cup of chicken broth
- ½ cup of coconut milk
- 1/2 cup of unsweetened plain Greek yogurt

**Cooking Instructions:**

1. Place garlic and ginger, in a food processor and blend until smooth; set it aside. Heat ghee or butter over medium heat.

2. Add onion, and cook until soft, for about 3 to 5 minutes. Add and mix in the garlic & ginger paste. Add coriander, garam masala, cumin, turmeric, and chili powder.

3. Stir until combined. Stir in diced chicken, and cook for about 5 minutes. Pour tomato sauce and chicken broth over chicken.

4. Heat until the broth starts to bubble, then cover, reduce heat, and simmer for about 15 minutes, stirring occasionally.

5. In a food processor add: almond butter, coconut milk and yogurt. Process until smooth. Stir the almond butter coconut milk mixture into the chicken and sauce.

6. Cover and simmer on low heat for about 10 to 12 minutes, stirring occasionally. Serve, can also serve over cauliflower rice.

Bruschetta Chicken

Preparation time: 10 minutes

Cooking time: 10 minutes

Gross time: 20 minutes

Serves: 2 to 4 people

**Recipe Ingredients:**

**Bruschetta:**

- 4 Roma tomatoes seeded and diced
- 3 cloves of garlic minced
- 3 tablespoons of olive oil
- 2 teaspoons of balsamic vinegar
- 2 tablespoons of fresh basil chopped
- 1 teaspoon of salt
- ¼ teaspoon of fresh cracked pepper

**Chicken:**

- 4 medium boneless skinless chicken breasts uniformly sized
- Salt and pepper
- 2 teaspoons of avocado or refined coconut oil

**Cooking Instructions:**

1. Stir together all bruschetta ingredients in a medium bowl and set it aside. If desired, gently pour out excess liquid after a few minutes, if tomatoes are very watery.

2. Heat 2 teaspoons of oil over medium heat. Season both sides of chicken breasts with plenty of salt and pepper.

3. Gently add chicken breasts to skillet without overcrowding. Cook the first side for about 8 minutes without moving.

4. Flip chicken breasts and cook second sides for about 2 to 4 minutes or until cooked through, for about 161 to 162°F internal temperature.

5. Transfer to a plate and let it rest for about 5 minutes. After resting chicken breasts for about 5 minutes.

6. Transfer chicken to serving plates and top generously with bruschetta. Serve immediately and Enjoy!

## Chicken Divan Casserole

Preparation time: 15 minutes

Cooking time: 45 minutes

Gross time: 60 minutes

Serves: 4 to 6 people

**Recipe Ingredients:**

- 3 cooked chicken breasts, cooled and cubed
- 1 package of frozen broccoli florets or chopped broccoli (at least 10 oz)
- 3 cups of grated cheddar cheese
- 1/3 Low-Carb Cream of Chicken Soup
- 1 cup of mayonnaise
- Juice of 1 lemon
- Salt and pepper

**Cooking Instructions:**

1. Pre-heat oven to 350°F. In a 9x13 baking dish, combine cooked chicken, frozen broccoli, and 1 ½ cups of grated cheese.

2. In a separate bowl, stir together cream of chicken soup, mayonnaise, lemon juice, and salt and pepper.

3. Pour soup/mayonnaise mixture over baking dish and stir to combine. Top with 1 ½ cups of grated cheese and cover with foil.

4. Bake at 350° for about 30 minutes, then remove foil and bake for another 20 minutes, or until cheese is bubbly.

5. Serve immediately and Enjoy!

## Pecan Crusted Chicken

Preparation time: 5 minutes

Cooking time: 20 minutes

Gross time: 25 minutes

Serves: 2 to 4 people

**Recipe Ingredients:**

- 4 chicken breasts or cutlets
- ½ tsp. of table salt
- ¼ tsp. of black pepper
- 1 ½ cups of finely chopped pecans cutlets use less than breasts
- 1 large egg lightly beaten
- 3 tbsp. of olive oil or coconut oil

**Cooking Instructions:**

1. Preheat oven to 350°F and sprinkle chicken with salt and pepper. Place pecans in a shallow bowl and egg in an additional shallow bowl.

2. Dip chicken in egg and then into pecans, pressing firmly to adhere. If pecans are too large they will not adhere properly.

3. Cook chicken in hot oil in a large nonstick skillet over medium-high heat. Cook until exterior is nicely browned and then transfer to cookie sheet in oven.

4. Cook until flesh is white and any juices run clear (165 internal temperature) this took about 10 minutes.

5. Cook until done, approximately for about 2 to 3 minutes per side. Serve immediately and Enjoy!

## Chicken Club Lettuce Wraps

Preparation time: 5 minutes

Cooking time: 10 minutes

Gross time: 15 minutes

Serves: 2 to 4 people

**Recipe Ingredients:**

- 3 chicken tenders or one chicken breast; seasoned cooked and diced
- ½ pint of grape tomatoes diced
- ½ avocado diced
- 4 slices of bacon cooked and diced
- 4 iceberg or romaine lettuce leaves
- 2 tbsp. of Dijon Mustard
- 2 tbsp. of sour cream
- ¼ tsp. of freshly ground black pepper

**Cooking Instructions:**

1. In a small bowl, whisk together mustard, sour cream and pepper. Set it aside for topping lettuce wraps.

2. Divide the diced chicken among the four lettuce leaves, then top with avocado, tomatoes, bacon, and Dijon dressing.

3. To eat, simply pick up the wrap like a taco, and enjoy!

# SOUP, STEW & SALAD RECIPES

## Chicken Enchilada Soup

Preparation time: 20 minutes

Cooking time: 3 hours 10 minutes

Gross time: 3 hours 30 minutes

Serves: 2 to 4 people

**Recipe Ingredients:**

- 2 tsp. of olive oil (10 ml)
- 1 red onion (110 g), peeled and finely chopped
- 2 tsp. of cumin powder (4 g)
- 1 tsp. of cayenne pepper (2 g)
- 2 cloves of garlic (6 g), peeled and finely chopped
- 4 chicken breasts (800 g), skinless and deboned
- 2 tsp. of dried oregano (2 g)
- 3 ½ cups of chicken broth (840 ml)
- ¾ can of diced tomatoes (300 g)
- 1 yellow bell pepper (120 g), chopped
- Salt and pepper to taste
- 2 slices tomato (45 g), halved to garnish
- 1 large avocado (200 g), diced to garnish
- Cilantro, finely chopped to garnish
- ½ red chili pepper (7 g), seeds removed and finely chopped to garnish

**Cooking Instructions:**

1. Chop the red onion and set aside 2 tablespoons to use as garnish. Cook onions in a pan with olive oil until soft and caramelized.

2. Halfway through, add the cumin, cayenne pepper, and garlic. Add the onions, chicken, and oregano to the slow cooker. Pour in the chicken broth and tomatoes.

3. Cover and cook for on high for about 2.5 hours. Add the bell pepper and cook for another 30 minutes. Shred the chicken.

4. Season with salt and pepper. If desired, garnish with a small slice tomato, avocado, cilantro, red chili, and onions, serve warm.

## Chicken and Cabbage Stew

Preparation time: 10 minutes

Cooking time: 1 hour

Gross time: 1 hour 10 minute

Serves: 2 to 4 people

**Recipe Ingredients:**

- 3 tbsp. (45 ml) of coconut oil, to cook with
- 2 chicken breasts, diced
- 4 slices bacon, diced
- ½ onion, diced
- ½ cabbage, sliced
- 3 cups (720 ml) of water or chicken broth
- Salt and pepper, to taste

**Cooking Instructions:**

1. Sauce the chicken, bacon, and onion in the coconut oil until the chicken is browned.

2. Add in the cabbage and water and bring to the boil. Cook for about 1 hour on low heat with the lid on. Add in salt and pepper, to taste.

3. Serve immediately and Enjoy!

## Chicken "Ramen" Soup

Preparation time: 10 minutes

Cooking time: 10 minutes

Gross time: 20 minutes

Serves: 1 to 3 people

**Recipe Ingredients:**

- 1 chicken breast, sliced
- 4 cups (960 ml) of chicken broth (or chicken bone broth)
- 2 eggs
- 1 zucchini, made into noodles
- 1 tbsp. of ginger, minced
- 2 cloves of garlic, peeled and minced
- 2 tbsp. (30 ml) of gluten-free tamari sauce or coconut aminos
- 3 tbsp. (45 ml) avocado oil, to cook with

**Cooking Instructions:**

1. Pan-fry the chicken slices in the avocado oil in a large frying pan until cooked and browned. Hard boil the 2 eggs and slice in half.

2. Add chicken broth to a large pot and simmer with the ginger, garlic, tamari sauce, and add in the zucchini noodles for 2 to 3 minutes to soften them.

3. Divide the broth into 2 bowls, top with the boil eggs and chicken breast slices.

4. Season with additional hot sauce or tamari sauce, to taste. Serve immediately and Enjoy!

## Homemade Thai chicken broth

Preparation time: 5 minutes

Cooking time: 8 hours

Gross time: 8 hours 5 minutes

Serves: 8 to 10 minutes

### Recipe Ingredients:

- 1 whole chicken
- 1 stalk of lemongrass, cut into large chunks
- 20 fresh basil leaves (10 for the slow cooker, and 10 for garnish)
- 5 thick slices of fresh ginger
- 1 lime
- 1 tbsp. of salt
- Additional salt to taste

### Cooking Instructions:

1. Place the chicken, lemongrass, 10 basil leaves, ginger, and salt into the slow cooker. Fill up the slow cooker with water.

2. Cook on low for 8-10 hours. Ladle the broth into a bowl, add in salt to taste, squeeze in fresh lime juice to taste, and garnish with chopped basil leaves.

3. Serve immediately and Enjoy!

Chicken Noodle Soup

Preparation time: 15 minutes

Cooking time: 15 minutes

Gross time: 30 minutes

Serves: 2 to 4 people

**Recipe Ingredients:**

- 3 cups of chicken broth
- 1 chicken breast, chopped into small pieces
- 2 tbsp. of avocado oil
- 1 stalk of celery, chopped
- 1 green onion, chopped
- ¼ cup of cilantro, finely chopped
- 1 zucchini, peeled
- Salt to taste.

**Cooking Instructions:**

1. Dice the chicken breast. Add the avocado oil into a saucepan and Sauté the diced chicken in there until cooked.

2. Add chicken broth to the same saucepan and simmer. Chop the celery and add it into the saucepan. Chop the green onions and add it into the saucepan.

3. Chop the cilantro and put it aside for the moment. Add zucchini noodles and cilantro to the pot.

4. Simmer for a few more minutes, add salt to taste, and serve immediately.

## Chicken Fajita Soup

Preparation time: 5 minutes

Cooking time: 5 hours

Gross time: 5 hours 5 minutes

Serve: 6 to 8 people

**Recipe Ingredients:**

- 1 ½ pounds of chicken breasts
- 1 (20-ounces) can of diced tomatoes, with juice
- 4 cups of chicken stock
- 1 (10-ounces) can of red enchilada sauce
- 1 (4-ounces) can of chopped green chilies
- 3 cloves of garlic, minced
- 1 large yellow onion, chopped small
- ½ red and ½ green bell peppers, diced
- 1 poblano pepper, diced (optional addition for more pepper flavor)
- 1 jalapeno pepper, diced small
- 1 tablespoon of chili powder
- 1 ½ teaspoon of paprika
- 1 teaspoon cumin
- ½ teaspoon salt
- ½ teaspoon of ground black pepper
- 1 teaspoon of onion powder
- 1 teaspoon of oregano (dried)
- ½ teaspoon of cayenne
- 1 bay leaf
- 1 or 2 avocados, cubed (for topping)
- 2 limes, juice of
- ¼ cup of cilantro, leaves chopped small

**Cooking Instructions**

1. Combine everything in your crock pot except: lime juice, cilantro and avocados. Cook on low setting in crock pot for about 5 to 6 hours.

2. Taste the stock during cooking and adjust seasoning as desired. Once chicken is cooked through (with an internal temperature of 160-degrees F).

3. Remove pieces and shred with a couple of forks and return shredded chicken to the crockpot.

4. Just before serving: Remove bay leaf, add cilantro, and the juice of two limes (about ¼ cup), serve in soup bowls, top with avocado slices.

5. Serve and enjoy!

## Asian Miso Soup Topped with Shrimp

Preparation time: 5 minutes

Cooking time: 5 minutes

Gross time: 10 minutes

Serves: 1 to 3 people

### Recipe Ingredients:

- 2 (3 ounces or 85 g) packs of shirataki noodles, drained
- 3 cups of chicken broth (600 ml) or bone broth
- 1 tbsp. of tahini sauce (15 ml)
- 1 tbsp. of gluten-free tamari sauce or coconut aminos (15 ml)
- ½ pound of shrimp (225 g), peeled
- 1 tsp. of sesame oil (5 ml)
- 2 tbsp. of lemon juice (30 ml)
- 2 green onions (10 g), sliced at an angle
- 1 cup of spinach (30 g), thinly sliced
- Dash of hot sauce (optional)

### Cooking Instructions:

1. Rinse the shirataki noodles very well, as per the packet instructions to eliminate the smell. It also helps to boil it up a bit and then rinse again.

2. Drain and set it aside. Heat the broth and add the tahini sauce and tamari sauce.

3. Once steaming hot, add the shrimp, sesame oil, and lemon juice and keep on the heat until you are certain the shrimp have cooked through.

4. Add the drained noodles into the broth along with the green onions and thinly sliced spinach and warm through.

5. Divide between 2 bowls and serve immediately with a dash of hot sauce.

Salmon Stew

Preparation time: 5 minutes

Cooking time: 20 minutes

Gross time: 25 minutes

Serves: 2 to 4 people

**Recipe Ingredients:**

- 32 ounces (or 1 liter) of chicken broth
- 3 (6 to 8ounces) of salmon filets
- 1 cup of parsley, chopped
- 3 cups of Swiss chard, roughly chopped
- 2 Italian squash, chopped
- 1 clove of garlic, crushed
- Juice from ½ a lemon
- Salt and pepper to taste
- 2 eggs

**Cooking Instructions:**

1. Pour the chicken broth into a pot and start heating it up.

2. While the broth is heating up, chop the vegetables and drop them along with the crushed garlic into the pot.

3. Then chop up the salmon into strips or chunks and drop into the pot. Add the lemon juice. Cook for about 10 minutes on a medium heat.

4. Crack 2 eggs into the pot and stir it up (make sure to break the yolk). Add salt and pepper to taste.

5. Serve immediately and Enjoy!

## Simple Coconut Seafood Soup

Preparation time: 15 minutes

Cooking time: 15 minutes

Gross time: 30 minutes

Serves: 2 to 4 people

**Recipe Ingredients:**

- 32 ounces of chicken stock
- 10 button of mushrooms (or other mushrooms), sliced
- ½ cup of kale, chopped
- 1 cup of romaine lettuce, chopped
- 4 tilapia filets, chopped into large chunks
- 10 shrimp/prawns
- 10 mussels, optional
- 1 cup of coconut cream (from the top of a refrigerated can of coconut milk)
- 1 tsp. of red boat fish sauce, optional
- Salt to taste, if needed

**Cooking instructions:**

1. Pour the chicken stock into a large pot and bring to the boil. Add in the mushrooms, kale, and romaine lettuce, and bring to the boil again.

2. Add in the tilapia pieces, the shrimp/prawns, and any other seafood, and bring to the boil again.

3. Boil for about 4 minutes until the shrimp/prawns have turned pink and the tilapia pieces are no longer translucent.

4. Add in the coconut cream, fish sauce (optional), and salt to taste. Stir to mix (but be careful not to break up the fish pieces too much).

5. Wait for it to just start boiling, then take off the heat and serve immediately.

## Spicy Halibut Tomato Soup

Preparation time: 15 minutes

Cooking time: 50 minutes

Overall time: 1 hour 5 minutes

Serves: 6 to 8 people

**Recipe Ingredients:**

- 1 teaspoon of olive oil
- 2 cloves of garlic minced
- ¼ cup of parsley fresh, chopped
- 3 tomatoes diced, without peel
- 10 anchovies canned in oil, minced
- 6 cups of vegetable broth 3 bouillon cubes + 6 cups water
- 1 teaspoon of salt
- 1 teaspoon of black pepper
- 1 teaspoon of red chili flakes
- 1 lb. of halibut filets fresh, chopped

**Cooking Instructions:**

1. In a large stockpot, heat olive oil over medium heat. Add garlic and half of the parsley, reserving the remainder for garnish.

2. Mix in tomatoes, anchovies, vegetable broth, salt, pepper, and red chili flakes. Increase heat to high and bring the pot to a boil.

3. Reduce heat to medium-low, cover the pot, and simmer for about 20 minutes. Remove lid and add halibut.

4. Replace cover and cook for an additional 8 to 10 minutes, or until fish easily flakes apart. Remove from heat and break down halibut into small pieces.

5. Mix to evenly distribute the fish. Serve garnished with the remaining fresh parsley.

### Creamy Leek & Salmon Soup

Preparation time: 5 minutes

Cooking time: 25 minutes

Gross time: 30 minutes

Serves: 2 to 4 people

**Recipe Ingredients:**

- 2 tablespoon of avocado oil
- 4 leeks, washed, trimmed and sliced into crescents
- 3 cloves of garlic, minced
- 6 cups of seafood OR chicken broth
- 2 teaspoons of dried thyme leaves
- 1 pounds of salmon, in bite size pieces
- 1 ¾ cup coconut milk
- Salt and pepper to taste (omit pepper for AIP)

**Cooking Instructions:**

1. Heat the avocado oil in a large saucepan or Dutch oven at a low-medium heat. Add the chopped leeks and garlic and cook until slightly softened.

2. Pour in the stock and add the thyme. Simmer for about 15 minutes and season to taste with salt and pepper.

3. Add the salmon and the coconut milk to the pan. Bring back up to a gentle simmer and cook until the fish is opaque and tender.

4. Serve immediately and Enjoy!

Thai Coconut Soup with Shrimp

Preparation time: 5 minutes

Cooking time: 30 minutes

Gross time: 35 minutes

Serve: 2 to 4 people

**Recipe Ingredients:**

**Broth:**

- 4 cups of chicken broth
- 1.5 cups of full fat coconut milk
- 3 kaffir lime leaves or zest of 1 organic lime
- 1-inch of fresh lemongrass cut in slices or 1 teaspoon dried lemongrass
- 1 cup of fresh cilantro
- 3 or 4 dried Thai chilies or 1 jalapeno sliced
- 1-inch of piece of fresh galangal root
- Lemongrass, galangal and chilis together here)
- 1 tsp. of sea salt

**Soup:**

- 100 grams of raw wild caught shrimp
- 1 tbsp. of coconut oil
- 30 grams of mushrooms (any kind) sliced.
- 30 grams red onion, sliced thinly
- 1 tbsp. of fish sauce or 1 anchovy finely smashed
- Juice of 1 lime
- 1 tbsp. of chopped cilantro to garnish

**Cooking Instructions:**

1. Put all ingredients in a sauce pan and simmer very lightly for about 20 minutes. Strain through a fine mesh colander and pour back into the pan.

2. Bring the broth back to a simmer, then add the shrimp or chicken and the fish sauce or anchovy. Add the sliced onion and the mushrooms.

3. Let simmer for about 10 minutes, until the meat is done. Add the lime juice and serve in bowls with the chopped cilantro as garnish.

Cheesy Zucchini Soup

Preparation time: 10 minutes

Cooking time: 20 minutes

Serves: 2 to 4 people

**Recipe Ingredients:**

- 2 tbsp. (30 ml) of coconut oil
- 1 medium onion (110 g), peeled and chopped
- 3 zucchinis (360 g), cut into chunks
- 2 cups (480 ml) of bone broth
- 1 tbsp. (8 g) of nutritional yeast
- Dash of freshly ground black pepper
- 1 tbsp. (15 ml) of coconut cream, for garnish
- 1 tbsp. of parsley, chopped, for garnish

**Cooking Instructions:**

1. Over medium heat, melt the coconut oil in a large pan. Add the onions and cook until soft. Add the zucchinis and bone broth and reduce to a simmer.

2. Partially cover the pan with a lid and cook until the zucchinis have completely cooked through. They should slide effortlessly off a fork when pierced.

3. Stir in the nutritional yeast and remove the pan from the heat. Use a hand blender or food processor to blitz the mixture to a fine soup puree.

4. Season with freshly ground black pepper. Serve garnished with a decorative drizzle of coconut cream and chopped parsley.

## Cabbage Soup

Preparation time: 15 minutes

Cooking time: 45 minutes

Gross time: 60 minutes

Serves: 2 to 4 people

**Recipe Ingredients:**

- 3 tbsp. (45 ml) of coconut oil, to cook with
- 1 small cabbage (green or purple), chopped
- 1 carrot, diced
- 3 stalks of celery, chopped
- ½ onion, chopped
- 1 tomato, diced
- 6 cups (1.5 l) of bone broth (or vegetable broth if vegan or vegetarian)
- 2 cloves of garlic, minced
- 2 tbsp. of parsley, chopped
- Salt and pepper, to taste

**Cooking Instructions:**

1. Add coconut oil to a large pot and heat up the pot. Sauté the cabbage, carrot, celery, and onion in the coconut oil until the vegetables are slightly browned.

2. Add the diced tomatoes and bone broth into the pot and bring to a boil. Then simmer for about 30 minutes until the cabbage is tender.

3. Add in the garlic and parsley and salt and pepper, to taste. Cook for about 5 more minutes and serve.

Spring Soup with Poached Egg

Preparation time: 5 minutes

Cooking time: 15 minutes

Serves: 1 to 3 people

**Recipe Ingredients:**

- 2 eggs
- 32 ounces (1 quart) of chicken broth
- 1 head of romaine lettuce, chopped
- Salt to taste

**Cooking instructions:**

1. Bring the chicken broth to a boil. Turn down the heat and poach the 2 eggs in the broth for 5 minutes (for a slightly-runny egg).

2. Remove the eggs and place each into a bowl. Add the chopped romaine lettuce into the broth and cook for a few minutes until slightly wilted.

3. Ladle the broth with the lettuce into the bowls. Serve immediately and Enjoy!

## Mint Avocado Chilled Soup

Preparation time: 5 minutes

Cooking time: 5 minutes

Gross time: 10 minutes

Serves: 1 to 3 people

**Recipe Ingredients:**

- 1 medium ripe avocado
- 2 romaine lettuce leaves
- 1 cup (240 ml) coconut milk, chilled
- 1 tbsp. (15 ml) of lime juice
- 20 fresh mint leaves
- Salt to taste

**Cooking Instructions:**

1. Place all the ingredients into a blender and blend really well. The soup should be thick but not as thick as a puree.

2. Chill in fridge for about 5 to 10 minutes. Serve immediately and Enjoy!

## Thai Beef and Broccoli Soup

Preparation time: 5 minutes

Cooking time: 40 minutes

Gross time: 45 minutes

Serves: 2 to 4 people

**Recipe Ingredients:**

- 2 tbsp. of avocado oil or fat of choice
- 1 onion, chopped
- 2 tbsp. of Thai green curry paste, adjust to taste
- 2-inch of knob ginger, minced
- 2 garlic cloves, minced
- 1 serrano pepper, minced
- 1 lb. of ground beef
- 3 tbsp. of coconut amino
- 2 tsp. of fish sauce
- ½ tsp. of salt
- ½ tsp. of black pepper
- 4 cups of beef bone broth or chicken stock
- 2 large stalks of broccoli, cut into florets
- 1 cup of full-fat canned coconut milk
- Cilantro, garnish

**Cooking Instructions:**

1. Add the oil and onions to a Dutch oven and cook for 10 minutes, or until the onions begin to turn golden.

2. Add the curry paste, ginger, garlic and serrano pepper and stir for a minute. Next, add the ground beef, coconut amino, fish sauce, salt and pepper and cook until the beef is nearly brown.

3. Add the broth, reduce the heat to low-medium. Cover the pot with a lid and cook for about 20 minutes. Add the broccoli florets and coconut milk to the pot.

4. Cover and cook for another 10 minutes. Remove the lid, increase heat to high and simmer for about 5 minutes. Garnish with cilantro.

## Turmeric Bone Broth

Preparation time: 5 minutes

Cooking time: 5 minutes

Gross time: 10 minutes

Serves: 1 to 3 people

**Recipe Ingredients**

- 1 cup (240 ml) of Keto bone broth
- 1 tsp. (2 g) of turmeric powder
- 1 tsp. (2 g) of ginger powder
- Dash of cumin powder
- Dash of pepper
- Salt to taste

**Cooking Instruction:**

1. Heat up the bone broth and whisk in the other ingredients.
2. Serve immediately and Enjoy!

## Bacon Cheeseburger Soup

Preparation time: 10 minutes

Cooking time: 50 minutes

Gross time: 60 minutes

Serves: 3 to 5 people

**Recipe Ingredients:**

- 5 slices of bacon
- 12 ounces of ground beef (80/20)
- 2 tablespoons of butter
- 3 cups of beef broth
- ½ teaspoon of garlic powder
- ½ teaspoon onion powder
- 2 teaspoon of brown mustard
- 1 ½ teaspoon of kosher salt
- ½ teaspoon of black pepper
- ½ teaspoon of red pepper flakes
- 1 teaspoon of cumin
- 1 teaspoon of chili powder
- 2 ½ tablespoon of tomato paste
- 1 medium dill pickle, diced
- 1 cup of shredded cheddar cheese
- 3 ounces of cream cheese
- ½ cup of heavy cream

**Cooking Instruction:**

1. Cook bacon in a pan until crispy, then set it aside. Add ground beef in the bacon fat and cook until browned on one side, flip and brown on other side.

2. Transfer beef to a pot, and move it to the sides. Add butter and spices to the pan and let the spices sweat for about 30 to 45 seconds.

3. Add beef broth, tomato paste, mustard, cheese, and pickles to the pot and let cook for a few minutes until melted. Cover pot and turn to low heat.

4. Cook for 20 to 30 minutes. Turn stove off, then finish with heavy cream and crumbled bacon. Stir well and serve.

# BEEF & PORK RECIPES

## Pork Egg Roll in A Bowl

Preparation time: 5 minutes

Cooking time: 25 minutes

Gross time: 30 minutes

Serves: 2 to 4 people

**Recipe Ingredients:**

- 2 tbsp. of sesame oil
- 3 cloves of garlic, minced
- ½ cup of onion, diced
- 5 green onions, sliced on a bias (white and green parts)
- 1 lb. of ground pork
- ½ tsp. of ground ginger (get it here)
- Sea salt and black pepper, to taste
- 1 tbsp. of Sriracha or garlic chili sauce, more to taste
- 14 oz. of bag coleslaw mix
- 3 tbsp. of coconut aminos or gluten free soy sauce(get it here)
- 1 tbsp. of rice vinegar (get it here)
- 2 tbsp. of toasted sesame seeds

**Cooking Instructions:**

1. Heat sesame oil in a large skillet over medium high heat. Add the garlic, onion, and white portion of the green onions.

2. Sauté until the onions are translucent and the garlic is fragrant. Add the ground pork, ground ginger, sea salt, black pepper and Sriracha.

3. Sauté until the pork is cooked through. Add the coleslaw mix, coconut aminos, and rice wine vinegar.

4. Sauté until the coleslaw is tender. Top with green onions and sesame seeds before serving. Serve and enjoy!

## Bacon Covered Meatloaf

Preparation time: 15 minutes

Cooking time: 50 minutes

Overall time: 1 hour 5 minutes

Serves: 10 to 12 people

**Recipe Ingredients:**

- 1 spring onion, sliced
- 2 cloves of garlic crushed
- 750 g of mince/ground beef
- 750 of g mince/ground pork
- 2 eggs - medium lightly beaten
- Handful fresh parsley chopped
- Handful fresh basil chopped
- 2 slices of bacon diced
- 2 tablespoons of sun-dried tomatoes chopped
- 2 teaspoons of dried oregano
- Salt and pepper to taste
- Vegetables of choice diced/grated/shredded
- 6 slices of bacon to cover the meatloaf
- Optional - if not paleo you can add 100g / 3.5 grated cheese of choice to the meatloaf mixture

**Cooking Instructions:**

1. Oil and line a baking tray before you start. Put all the ingredients in a large mixing bowl.

2. Mix together with your hands until all the ingredients are thoroughly incorporated together.

3. Form into a large meatloaf shape on the lined baking tray. Cover with the bacon slices and sprinkle on parmesan cheese.

4. Bake at 180C/350F for 50 minutes or until thoroughly cooked in the centre. Serve immediately and Enjoy!

## Spaghetti Squash with Meat Sauce

Preparation time: 10 minutes

Cooking time: 1 hour

Gross time: 1 hour 10 minutes

Serves: 2 to 4 people

**Recipe Ingredients:**

- 1 spaghetti squash, split lengthwise and seeded
- ½ lb. ground pork (or beef, turkey, or chicken)
- 15 oz. of can of fire-roasted diced tomatoes
- 1 tbsp. of Italian seasoning

**Cooking Directions:**

1. Preheat oven to 350°F and season cut squash with salt and brush with a little avocado oil. Place cut side down in a baking dish. Bake for about 40 minutes.

2. The time may vary a little depending on the size of the squash. Check after about 35 minutes. It should be tender and let it cool.

3. Using a fork, pull strands out of squash halves. While the squash is baking, prepare the simple meat sauce. In a skillet, cook pork until there is no pinker.

4. Add the tomatoes and Italian seasoning and allow to boil. Reduce heat and let simmer until squash is ready.

5. Spoon cooked spaghetti squash into 2 to 3 bowls. Top with meat sauce. Season with salt if necessary. Enjoy!

Ground Pork Tacos

Preparation time: 5 minutes

Cooking time: 5 minutes

Gross time: 10 minutes

Serves: 2 to 4 people

**Recipe Ingredients:**

- 400 grams of ground pork (about 13 oz.)
- ½ teaspoon of garlic powder
- ½ teaspoon of onion powder
- ½ teaspoon of sea salt
- 1/8 teaspoon of cumin
- 1/8 teaspoon of ground pepper
- 5 tablespoons of salsa
- 5 or more lettuce leaves (I used Boston Red Leaf Lettuce)
- Taco toppings like diced green peppers/red peppers/avocado/onions etc.

**Cooking Instructions:**

1. In a small bowl, mix using your hands, the ground pork and all the seasoning (except for the salsa). Place the meat in a frying pan and turn the heat to medium.

2. Constantly stir the meat making sure to breakup any large pieces. Once the meat is cooked drain the fat from the pan.

3. Add the salsa and mix. Place the meat on the lettuce wraps and top with your favorite taco toppings.

4. Serve immediately and Enjoy!

## Homemade "Hungarian" Sausage

Preparation time: 5 minutes

Cooking time: 20 minutes

Gross time: 25 minutes

Serves: 2 to 4 people

**Recipe Ingredients:**

- 1 pound of ground pork (preferably pastured)
- ½ tsp. garlic powder
- 1 ½ teaspoons paprika
- 1 teaspoon of salt
- 1 tablespoon of cooking fat (tallow or coconut oil are great)

**Cooking Instructions:**

1. Mix herbs and ground pork in a small bowl, make sure the spices are well mixed in. Form four patties.

2. Heat a skillet over medium-high heat. Add cooking fat to skillet. Add sausage patties to skillet.

3. Cook on the first side for approximately 10 minutes. Cook until you can see the meat cooking on the edges and the underneath looks a little browned.

4. Flip and cook on the second side for about 7 to 8 minutes, or until cooked through.

5. Serve immediately and Enjoy!

## Pork and Cashew Stir-Fry

Preparation time: 5 minutes

Cooking time: 10 minutes

Gross time: 15 minutes

Serves: 1 to 3 people

**Recipe Ingredients:**

- ½ pounds (225 g) of pork tenderloin, sliced thin
- 1 egg, whisked
- 1 bell pepper, diced
- 1 green onion, diced
- 1/3 cup (40 g) of cashews
- 1 tbsp. (5 g) of fresh ginger, grated
- 3 cloves of garlic, minced
- 1 tsp. (5 ml) of Chinese chili oil (optional)
- 1 tbsp. (15 ml) of sesame oil (optional)
- 2 tbsp. (30 ml) of gluten-free tamari sauce or coconut aminos
- Salt to taste
- Avocado oil to cook with

**Cooking Instructions:**

1. Place the avocado oil into a frying pan and cook the whisked egg and place it aside on a plate.

2. Add additional avocado oil into the frying pan and cook the pork. Then, add in the pepper, onion, and cashews.

3. Sauté until the pork is fully cooked, then, add back in the cooked egg.

4. Then add in the ginger, garlic, chili oil, sesame oil, tamari sauce, and salt to taste. Serve immediately and Enjoy!

Chili Beef

Preparation time: 10 minutes

Cooking time: 2 hours 30 minutes

Gross time: 2 hours 40 minutes

Serve: 2 to 4 people

**Recipe Ingredients:**

- 1.25 pounds of ground beef
- 8 ounces of tomato paste
- 1 ½ tomatoes chopped
- 1 red bell pepper chopped
- 2/4 cup of onion chopped
- 2 celery sticks chopped
- 1 ½ tsp. of cumin
- 1 ½ tsp. of chili powder
- ½ tsp. of pepper
- 1 ½ tsp. of salt
- ¾ cup of water add more if needed

**Cooking Instructions:**

1. Brown meat in fry pan. Once almost finished, drain off fat and sprinkle ½ teaspoon of salt over meat.

2. Add onions and peppers to a pan, continue to cook for 2 minutes. Combine cooked meat, onions, peppers, tomatoes, celery, water, and tomato paste in large pot.

3. Stir spices into pot and allow to boil, then reduce heat to low-medium and let simmer for about 1 to 2 hours, stirring every 30 minutes or so.

4. Serve immediately and Enjoy!

## Pan-Fried Pork Tenderloin

Preparation time: 5 minutes

Cooking time: 20 minutes

Gross time: 25 minutes

Serves: 1 to 3 people

**Recipe Ingredients:**

- 1 pound of pork tenderloin
- Salt and pepper to taste
- 1 tbsp. of coconut oil

**Cooking Instructions:**

1. Cut the 1 pound of pork tenderloin in half (to create 2 equal shorter halves). Place the 1 tablespoon of coconut oil into a frying pan on a medium heat.

2. After the coconut oil melts, place the 2 pork tenderloin pieces into the pan. Leave the pork to cook on its side.

3. Once that side is cooked, turn using tongs to cook the other sides. Keep turning and cooking until the pork looks cooked on all sides.

4. Cook all sides of the pork until the meat thermometer shows an internal temperature of just below 145°F.

5. The pork will keep on cooking a bit after you take it out of the pan. Let the pork sit for a few minutes and then slice into 1-inch thick slices with a sharp knife.

6. Serve immediately and Enjoy!

## Cheesy Mexican Taco Skillet

Preparation time: 10 minutes

Cooking time: 20 minutes

Gross time: 30 minutes

Serves: 2 to 4 people

**Recipe Ingredients:**

- 1 tbsp. of avocado oil
- 1 lb. of ground beef
- ½ white onion, diced (95g)
- ½ bell pepper, diced (100g)
- 1 (4-ounces) can of green chilis
- 3 tbsp. of taco seasoning
- 2 Roma tomatoes, seeded and diced (56g)
- 12 oz. of cauliflower rice
- 1 cup of shredded Mexican blend cheese

**Toppings:**

- 1 avocado, diced
- Sliced jalapeño
- Sour cream
- Cilantro

**Cooking Instructions:**

1. Heat the oil in a large cast iron skillet over medium high heat. Once hot add in the beef and cook while crumbling with a wooden spoon until it starts to brown.

2. Add in the onion, bell pepper, and taco seasoning and cook for about 3 minutes or until the onion and pepper starts to soften.

3. Stir in the green chiles and tomatoes along with the cauliflower rice. Cook for about 5 to 7 minutes until most of the moisture has evaporated.

4. Sprinkle with cheese and cover just until melted, about 2 minutes. Top with desired toppings and serve.

## Mu Shu Pork

Preparation time: 15 minutes

Cooking time: 15 minutes

Gross time: 30 minutes

Serves: 1 to 3 people

**Recipe Ingredients:**

- ½ pound of pork tenderloin, cut into small thin 1-inch long strips
- 3 eggs, whisked
- 15 Napa cabbage leaves, chopped into thin strips
- 1 cup of shiitake mushrooms, sliced
- 1 (8 ounces) can of sliced bamboo shoots
- ½ tsp. of freshly grated ginger
- 1 tbsp. of coconut aminos
- ½ tsp. of apple cider vinegar
- Salt to taste
- Coconut oil to cook in
- ¼ cup scallions (for garnish)
- Lettuce leaves to serve in (optional)

**Cooking Instructions:**

1. Add 1 tablespoon of coconut oil to a skillet on medium heat. Add a little bit of salt to the whisked eggs and pour the mixture into the skillet.

2. Let it cook undisturbed into a pancake. Flip the egg pancake once it's cooked most of the way through. Cook for a few more minutes.

3. Place on a cutting board and cut into thin 1-inch long strips. Cook the pork in a teaspoon of coconut oil. Stir with a spatula to make sure the strips don't clump together.

4. Once the pork is cooked, add in the strips of eggs, sliced mushrooms, sliced Napa cabbage, and bamboo shoots. Add in the ginger, coconut aminos, and apple cider vinegar.

5. Cook until the cabbage and mushrooms are soft. Then add salt to taste. Sprinkle the scallions on top for garnish and serve in lettuce cups or by itself.

## Spicy Pork with Kelp Noodles

Preparation time: 5 minutes

Cooking time: 15 minutes

Gross time 20 minutes

Serves: 2 to 4 people

**Recipe Ingredients:**

- 1 ½ lb. of pork tenderloin sliced thin
- 1 tbsp. of olive or avocado oil
- 2 cloves of garlic minced
- 1 medium cucumber sliced
- 12 oz. of package kelp noodles
- ½ tsp. of red pepper flakes
- 2 tbsp. of rice vinegar
- 2 tsp. of sesame oil
- 1 tsp. of coconut aminos or soy aminos
- ½ tsp. of ginger minced
- Salt and pepper to taste

**Cooking Instructions:**

1. Brown sliced pork in skillet with oil and garlic. Stir in sliced cucumber and kelp noodles.

2. Season with pepper flakes, vinegar, sesame oil, aminos, ginger, salt, and pepper.

3. Cover and cook another 5 to 7 minutes. Serve immediately and Enjoy!

## Apple Dijon Pork Chops

Preparation time: 5 minutes

Cooking time: 10 minutes

Gross time: 15 minutes

Serves: 1 to 3 people

**Recipe Ingredients:**

- 2 pork chops (320 g)
- 4 tbsp. of ghee (60 ml)
- 2 tbsp. of applesauce (30 ml)
- 2 tbsp. of ghee (30 ml)
- 2 tbsp. of Dijon mustard (30 ml)
- Salt and pepper, to taste

**Cooking Instructions:**

1. Melt the 4 tablespoons of ghee in a large pan. Add in the pork chops. Using tongs, position the pork chops on its side so that the fat cooks in the ghee first.

2. This makes browns and renders the fat a bit. Then once the fat is a bit crispy and browned, lay the pork chops flat in the ghee.

3. Cook for about 3 to 4 minutes on each side. Check using a meat thermometer that the internal temperature of the pork reaches 145°F.

4. When you cut into the pork chops, you'll find it has a medium rare pink inside. If you prefer your pork chops more cooked, then just leave it in there for longer.

5. Meanwhile, mix the applesauce, melted ghee, and mustard together well. Serve the pork chops with the sauce and season with salt and pepper to taste.

## Pork Chops & Cabbage

Preparation time: 5 minutes

Cooking time: 15 minutes

Overall time: 20 minutes

Serves: 1 to 3 people

**Recipe Ingredients:**

**The Pork Chops:**

- 2 boneless pork chops
- 1/8 teaspoon of coriander ground
- 1/8 teaspoon of garlic powder
- 1/8 teaspoon of sea salt
- 1 teaspoon of ghee

**The Cabbage:**

- 6 ounces of cabbage sliced into strips
- 1 tablespoon of apple cider vinegar
- ¼ cup of chicken broth
- 1/8 teaspoon of red chili flakes
- Sea salt to taste

**Cooking Instructions:**

1. Season each side of pork chops with coriander, garlic powder, and sea salt. Melt ghee in a cast-iron skillet over medium heat.

2. Cook pork chops for about 4 to 5 minutes on each side, or until they reach the desired temperature (145°F for medium rare or 160°F for medium).

3. Let it rest for about 5 minutes prior to slicing. In a medium skillet, bring cabbage, vinegar, broth, chili flakes, and sea salt to a boil over high heat.

4. Stir occasionally, cooking until the liquid has cooked off and the edges of the cabbage begin to brown.

5. Serve pork chops sliced with cabbage on the side and Enjoy!

## Korean Ground Beef Stir Fry

Preparation time: 10 minutes

Cooking time: 10 minutes

Gross time: 20 minutes

Serves: 3 to 5 people

**Recipe Ingredients:**

- 1 lb. of lean ground beef 90% lean
- 3 garlic cloves minced
- 1 tbsp. of olive oil
- 1 red bell pepper diced
- 1 zucchini sliced
- ½ cup of sugar snap peas
- ½ cup of shredded carrots
- 8 oz. of mushrooms sliced
- ½ cup of packed brown sugar
- ½ cup of reduced-sodium soy sauce
- 1 tbsp. of sesame oil
- ½ tsp. of ground ginger
- ¼ tsp. of crushed red pepper flakes
- ½ tsp. of pepper
- Sliced green onions and sesame seeds for garnish

**Cooking Instructions:**

1. In a large skillet cook the ground beef and garlic breaking it into crumbles over medium heat until no longer pink.

2. Remove the ground beef and set aside on a plate. Drain the grease and add 1 tablespoon of olive oil to the skillet.

3. Add bell pepper, zucchini, snap peas, carrots, and mushrooms. Sauté for about 2 to 3 minutes or until tender and add the ground back to the skillet.

4. In a small bowl whisk brown sugar, soy sauce, sesame oil, ginger, red pepper flakes and pepper.

5. Pour over the ground beef and let simmer for another minute or two. Serve over hot rice and garnish with green onions and sesame seeds.

6. Serve and enjoy!

## Cajun pork with Peppers and Tomatoes

Preparation time: 5 minutes

Cooking time: 20 minutes

Gross time: 25 minutes

Serves: 1 to 3 people

**Recipe Ingredients:**

- 1 pound of Cajun shredded pork
- 2 bell peppers, sliced
- 1 onion, sliced (optional)
- 1 14 ounces (400g) can of diced tomatoes (or use 2–3 fresh tomatoes)
- 4 cloves of garlic, minced
- Salt to taste
- Coconut oil to cook with

**Cooking Instructions:**

1. Sauté the bell peppers and onions in 1 tablespoon of coconut oil.

2. Once the bell peppers and onions are soft, add in the shredded pork followed by the tomatoes.

3. Simmer for 5 more minutes, then add in the minced garlic and season with salt to taste.

4. Cook for 2 more minutes. Serve immediately and Enjoy!

## Dry Rub Pork Spare Ribs

Preparation time: 15 minutes

Cooking time: 3 hours 30 minutes

Overall time: 3 hours 45 minutes

Serves: 2 to 4 people

**Recipe Ingredients:**

- 2 tbsp. of Cacao
- 1 tbsp. of coriander
- ½ tsp. of cumin
- ½ tsp. of cinnamon
- ½ tsp. of chili powder
- ½ tsp. Of black pepper
- 1 tbsp. of sea salt
- 2 racks ribs

**Cooking Instructions:**

1. Preheat your oven to 350°F and throw all the ingredients into a bowl and mix with a spoon until well blended.

2. Lightly apply this rub to both sides of your rack until it is well coated. Next take two sheets of aluminum foil and sandwich the ribs.

3. Place them in your oven to bake for about 3 to 3.25 hours. The meat should be falling off the bone by the time they are done.

4. Serve immediately and Enjoy!

## Cheeseburger Meatloaf

Preparation time: 15 minutes

Cooking time: 30 minutes

Overall time: 45 minutes

Serves: 2 to 4 people

**Recipe Ingredients:**

- 1 ¼ pounds of ground beef I use 90% lean
- Cooking spray
- 2 tsp. of olive oil
- ½ cup of onion finely diced
- ½ cup of cooked and crumbled bacon
- ¼ cup of panko breadcrumbs
- 1 tbsp. of yellow mustard
- 1 tbsp. of Worcestershire sauce
- ¾ tsp. of salt
- ½ tsp. of pepper
- 1 egg
- ½ cup of cheddar cheese cut into small cubes
- ¼ cup of ketchup
- 1 tbsp. of chopped parsley optional

**Cooking Instructions:**

1. Preheat the oven to 350°F and line a sheet pan with foil and coat with cooking spray. Heat the olive oil in a small pan over medium heat.

2. Add the onion and cook for about 4 to 5 minutes or until golden brown. Remove from the heat and stir in the mustard and Worcestershire sauce.

3. In a large bowl, combine the onion mixture, beef, bacon, panko breadcrumbs, salt, pepper, egg, 2 tablespoons of water and cheddar cheese.

4. Mix together until well blended. Form 4 individual meatloaves and place on prepared sheet pan. Spread 1 tablespoon of ketchup over each meatloaf.

5. Bake for about 20 to 25 minutes or until cooked through. Sprinkle with parsley if desired, and serve.

## Jamaican Jerk Pork Roast

Preparation time: 5 minutes

Cooking time: 3 hours

Overall time: 3 hours 5 minutes

Serves: 10 to 12 hours

**Recipe Ingredients:**

- 4 pounds of pork shoulder
- ¼ cup of Jamaican Jerk spice blend (no sugar)
- 1 tablespoon of olive oil
- ½ cup of beef stock or broth

**Cooking Instructions:**

1. Rub the roast with olive oil and coat with Jamaican Jerk spice blend. Sear the meat on all sides in a heavy bottomed pot. Add 1 cup of beef broth.

2. Cover and simmer on the stovetop on low heat for 4 hours, or bake in the oven at 375 degrees for 3 hours or until the meat is tender and falling apart.

3. Shred, serve immediately and enjoy!

## San Choy Bau

Preparation time: 10 minutes

Cooking time: 20 minutes

Gross time: 30 minutes

Serves: 2 to 4 people

**Recipe Ingredients:**

- 1 tbsp. of sesame oil
- 1 clove of garlic crushed
- 2 tsp. of ginger finely chopped
- 1 lb. of ground pork
- 3 scallions thinly sliced
- 1/3 cup of Keto Sweet Soy Sauce
- ¼ cup of bamboo shoots chopped
- ¼ tsp. of white pepper ground
- ¼ tsp. of xanthan gum
- Salt to taste
- ½ cup bean sprouts
- 12 small romaine lettuce leaves
- 2 tsp. of sesame seeds
- Fresh lime to serve

**Cooking Instructions:**

1. Place a large saucepan over high heat and add the sesame oil, garlic, and ginger, and Sauté for about 2 to 3 minutes until it is fragrant.

2. Add the ground pork. Break up the pork and cook until browned. Add the scallions, Keto Sweet Soy, bamboo shoots, and pepper and mix well.

3. Bring to a simmer, then sprinkle over the xanthan gum. Continue to cook, whilst stirring, until the sauce has thickened. Remove from the heat.

4. Taste and add salt, if needed. Stir through half of the cilantro. Place the lettuce cups onto your serving place and spoon the mixture evenly between them.

5. Top with the remaining cilantro, the bean sprouts, and sesame seeds. Serve immediately with a wedge of lime.

## Beef Cheeks

Preparation time: 5 minutes

Cooking time: 8 hours

Gross time: 8 hours 5 minutes

Serves 3 to 5 people

**Recipe Ingredients:**

- 1 orange, zest only
- 2 scallions, cut into 1in lengths
- 3 cloves of garlic, sliced
- 2-inch piece of fresh ginger, sliced
- ½ cup of Chinese cooking wine
- 1 cup of tamari sauce
- ⅓ cup of Sorkin brown sweetener
- 1 tbsp. of sesame oil
- 3-star anise
- 1 cinnamon stick
- 4 beef cheeks (2 ½ pounds)

**Cooking Instructions:**

1. Peel thick strips of the zest from the orange, using a vegetable peeler. Place in your slow cooker.

2. Add the scallions, garlic, ginger, cooking wine, tamari, sweetener, sesame oil, star anise and cinnamon to your slow cooker. Stir until the sweetener has dissolved.

3. Add the beef cheeks and coat in the sauce. Cook on low for about 8 hours. Serve the beef cheeks with a little cooking broth and a side of cauliflower rice.

# FISH & SEAFOOD RECIPES

### Steamed Clams

Preparation time: 3 minutes

Cooking time: 10 minutes

Gross time 13 minutes

Serves: 2 to 4 people

**Recipe Ingredients:**

- 1 lb. steamer-sized clams in shell small, ~68g without shell
- 3 tbsp. of unsalted butter
- 1 clove of garlic minced
- 10 fresh basil leaves whole
- ½ cup of chicken broth

**Cooking Instructions:**

1. Melt butter in large saucepan, one with a tight fitting lid, over medium heat. Add garlic, basil leaves, and chicken broth to the saucepan

2. Allow to boil over medium-high heat. Mix in clams and cover with tight fitting lid, leaving heat on medium-high.

3. Steam for about 7 to 8 minutes without removing the lid. While clams are steaming, shake pan over heat to evenly coat the shellfish.

4. Remove lid, if sauce looks thin, leave pan over heat without lid until sauce is desired consistency.

5. Add an additional tablespoon of butter to the pan if desired and fits your macros. Remove from heat when sauce reaches desired consistency.

6. Discard any clams that have not opened and serve immediately.

## Spicy Mussels in Tomato Chorizo Broth

Preparation time: 5 minutes

Cooking time: 15 minutes

Overall time: 20 minutes

Serves: 4 to 6 people

**Recipe Ingredients:**

- 1 pound of chorizo or other spicy sausage casings removed
- 3 garlic cloves minced
- ¼ teaspoon of red pepper flakes
- 1 (14- ounces) can of diced tomatoes
- 1 cup of Aphotic White Winemaker's Blend
- ¼ teaspoon of dried thyme
- 2 pounds of mussels cleaned and debearded
- Salt and pepper to taste

**Cooking Instructions:**

1. In a large pot or Dutch oven set over medium heat, brown sausage until cooked through, breaking up any chunks with the back of a wooden spoon.

2. Using a slotted spoon, remove sausage to a paper towel-lined plate to drain, leaving drippings in pan. Add garlic and red pepper flakes to pot.

3. Cook until fragrant, for about 2 minute. Add tomatoes, wine, and dried thyme and turn heat to medium high.

4. Bring to a boil and add mussels. Cover and cook for about 3 minutes. Remove lid, stir gently and re-cover.

5. Cook another 3 to 4 minutes, or until most mussels have opened (discard any that do not open). Remove mussels from pot with a slotted spoon or skimmer.

6. Return sausage to pot, season broth with salt and pepper and bring back to a boil for a few minutes until somewhat thickened.

7. Serve by placing mussels in large bowls and spooning sauce over.

## Garlic Lemon Butter Crab Legs

Preparation time: 10 minutes

Cooking time: 5 minutes

Overall time: 15 minutes

Serves: 1 to 3 people

**Recipe Ingredients:**

- 1 pound of king crab legs
- ½ stick salted butter, melted (4 tablespoons)
- 3 cloves of garlic, minced
- 1 tbsp. of chopped parsley
- ½ tbsp. of lemon juice
- Lemon slices

**Cooking Instructions:**

1. Preheat oven to 375°F. Thaw the crab legs if they are frozen. Using a sharp knife or a pair of a scissors, slice or cut the crab legs into halves to expose the flesh.

2. Arrange them evenly on a baking sheet or tray. Melt the butter in a microwave, for about 30 seconds. Add the garlic, parsley and lemon juice to the melted butter.

3. Stir to mix well. Drizzle and spread the butter mixture on the crab. Save some for dipping. Bake the crab legs in the oven for about 5 minutes.

4. Serve immediately with the remaining garlic lemon butter and lemon slices. Squeeze some lemon juice on the crab before eating.

## Soft Shell Crab

Preparation time: 8 minutes

Cooking time: 8 minutes

Overall time: 16 minutes

Serves: 1 to 3 people

**Recipe Ingredients:**

- 8 soft shell crabs (2 packages)
- ½ cup of powdered Parmesan
- 2 eggs, beaten
- 4 tbsp. of Carolina BBQ sauce

**Cooking Instructions:**

1. Heat a cast iron skillet with ½ cup lard or tallow to medium high heat. Pat the crab dry with paper towel.

2. Place the powdered parmesan into a large shallow dish. Place the beaten eggs into another large shallow dish.

3. Dip the crab into the eggs and tap, just so the crab has a light coating. Dip into the parmesan and use your hands to coat the crab well.

4. Drop 3 to 4 crabs into the hot oil. Cook for about 2 minutes, flip and cook another 2 minutes or until crab is cooked through.

5. Repeat with remaining crabs. While the crab cooks, prepare my Carolina BBQ sauce and serve with delicious crispy crab.

6. Serve immediately and enjoy!

## Salmon in Foil Packets with Pesto

Preparation time: 5 minutes

Cooking time: 15 minutes

Overall time: 20 minutes

Serves: 2 to 4 people

**Recipe Ingredients:**

- 1 lb. of salmon fillet (or four 4 ounce fillets)
- 2 tbsp. of olive oil
- ½ tsp. of kosher salt
- 1/8 tsp. of ground black pepper
- 20 cherry tomatoes
- ½ cup of dry white wine
- ¼ cup of prepared basil pesto
- Optional cauliflower rice for serving

**Cooking Instructions:**

1. Place the salmon on a sheet of tin foil that is large enough to wrap completely over itself to cover the salmon and seal in the steam.

2. Season the salmon with salt and pepper, then drizzle with olive oil. Place the tomatoes around the salmon.

3. Fold up the edges of the foil around it to create a 1-inch rim to trap the moisture inside. Pour the white wine into the foil around the salmon and tomatoes.

4. Fold the extra foil over the top of the salmon packet and lightly crimp to create a mostly sealed package.

5. Cook on a preheated grill (to about 400°F) over indirect heat for 10 minutes. Remove from the grill and keep covered five minutes.

6. Lift up the top layer of foil and brush the cooked salmon with the pesto. Serve warm with cauliflower rice if desired.

## Salmon Roasted in Butter

Preparation time: 5 minutes

Cooking time: 15 minutes

Gross time: 20 minutes

**Recipe Ingredients:**

- ¼ cup of unsalted butter
- 3 tablespoon of minced fresh dill
- 4 (6 ounces) skin-on salmon fillets (I recommend using thicker fillets)
- Salt and freshly ground black pepper
- 1 teaspoon of minced garlic
- 1 teaspoon of minced fresh parsley
- Lemon wedges or lemon zest, for serving

**Cooking Instructions:**

1. Preheat oven to 475ºF and place butter in small roasting dish. Sprinkle dill evenly across.

2. Place in oven and heat until butter has melted and dill is sizzling, for about 4 to 5 minutes. Remove pan from oven and place fillets skin-side up.

3. Return to oven and roast 4 minutes and remove from oven. Pull skin from salmon Season the now skinless side with salt and pepper.

4. Carefully flip fillets and season opposite side with salt and pepper. Sprinkle garlic into melted butter around salmon.

5. Return to oven and cook to desired doneness, for about 3 to 4 minutes longer. Plate salmon and spoon butter in pan over salmon.

6. Sprinkle with parsley and serve warm with lemon zest or lemon wedges for spritzing.

## Grilled Salmon with Creamy Pesto Sauce

Preparation time: 15 minutes

Cooking time: 10 minutes

Gross time: 25 minutes

Serves: 2 to 4 people

**Recipe Ingredients:**

- 5 (6 ounces) skin on or skinless salmon fillets
- Olive oil, for brushing salmon and grill
- Salt and freshly ground black pepper
- 4 ounces of cream cheese, diced into small cubes
- ¼ cup of milk
- 3 tablespoons of homemade or store-bought pesto, plus more for serving*

**Cooking Instructions:**

1. Preheat a grill over medium-high heat to about 425°F and brush both sides of salmon with olive oil (1 tablespoon total).

2. Season both sides with salt and pepper. Brush grill grates with oil and grill salmon about 3 minutes per side or to desired doneness.

3. While salmon is grilling, heat cream cheese with milk in a saucepan set over medium heat, stirring constantly until melted, for about 1 to 2 minutes.

4. Remove from heat and stir in pesto. Serve salmon warm with creamy pesto sauce. Spoon about 1 tsp. pesto over creamy pesto sauce for added color and flavor.

Cajun Salmon Patties

Preparation time: 5 minutes

Cooking time: 5 minutes

Gross time: 10 minutes

Serves: 2 to 4 people

**Recipe Ingredients:**

- 14 ounces can of pink salmon, drained with bones removed
- 2 ounces of smoked salmon (nova or lox style), roughly chopped
- 1 egg
- 3 tablespoons of Cilantro Lime dressing
- 1/3 cup of almond flour
- 2 tablespoons fresh parsley, chopped
- 1 teaspoon of Cajun seasoning
- 2 tablespoons avocado oil (or light olive oil) for frying

**Cooking Instructions:**

1. Beat the egg and Cilantro Lime dressing in a medium bowl. Add the salmon, almond flour, parsley and Cajun seasoning.

2. Stir gently until combined. Form into eight 2.5 inch patties. Heat the oil in a non-stick Sauté pan over medium heat.

3. Cook the patties in batches for about 2 minutes per side (until golden brown.) Remove cooked patties to a paper-towel lined plate.

4. Continue to warm until serving. Serve with Hidden Valley Ranch Cilantro Lime dressing and wedges of lemon if desired.

## Grilled Swordfish Skewers

Preparation time: 5 minutes

Cooking time: 10 minutes

Gross time: 15 minutes

Serves: 2 to 4 people

**Recipe Ingredients:**

- 1 pound of swordfish, cut into 1 inch cubes
- 16 cherry tomatoes
- Salt and pepper
- 1 teaspoon of olive oil to coat
- ¼ cup of pesto
- ¼ cup of mayonnaise

**Cooking Instructions:**

1. Divide the swordfish cubes into four equal portions. Alternate the swordfish with the cherry tomatoes on your skewers.

2. Brush with olive oil and season with salt and pepper. Preheat the grill for at least 5 minutes, then, carefully place your skewers on the hot grill.

3. Cook for about 1 minute per (four) sides of your cubes – a little longer if your swordfish pieces are really thick.

4. Serve warm or chilled with a salad. Combine the pesto and mayonnaise in a small bowl and stir well.

5. Serve with the skewers and enjoy!

## Almond and Parmesan Crusted Fish

Preparation time: 5 minutes

Cooking time: 40 minutes

Gross time: 45 minutes

Serves: 2 to 4 people

**Recipe Ingredients:**

- 1 pound (450 g) of Alaska Pollock, frozen
- 3 ounces (75 g) of salted butter, softened
- 2/3 cup (160 ml) of almond flour
- 2/3 cup (160 ml) of freshly grated Parmesan
- 2 tsp. of Italian herb seasoning
- Optional: to taste unrefined sea salt OR Himalayan salt

**Cooking Instructions:**

1. Preheat the oven to 350°F. Place the fish fillets into a glass or ceramic baking dish.

2. Combine the butter, almond flour (or crushed pork rinds), Parmesan, herb seasoning and the salt (if using) in a medium bowl.

3. Mix with an electric mixer until well-combined. Press the topping evenly on top of the fish fillets.

4. Bake in the preheated oven for about 35 to 40 minutes, or until the juices run clear and the topping is golden brown.

5. Serve immediately and Enjoy!

## Thai Seafood Chowder

Preparation time: 5 minutes

Cooking time: 30 minutes

Overall time: 35 minutes

Serves: 4 to 6 people

**Recipe Ingredients:**

- 2 tablespoons of avocado oil
- ¼ cup of diced onion
- Salt and pepper
- 2 stalks of celery chopped
- 1 jalapeño seeded and diced
- 2 tablespoons of green Thai curry paste
- 3 cups of chicken broth
- 1 (15- ounce) can of full fat coconut milk
- 1 red pepper julienned
- ½ head cabbage roughly chopped
- 1 pound of wild pacific cod cut into 1 inch chunks
- ½ pound of raw shrimp peeled and deveined
- ½ pound of raw calamari rings and tentacles
- 2 tablespoons of fish sauce
- 2 tablespoon of fresh lime juice
- ¼ cup of chopped fresh cilantro

**Cooking Instructions:**

1. In a large stock pot over medium heat, heat oil until shimmering. Add onion and a pinch of salt and pepper, and sauté until translucent, for about 4 minutes.

2. Add celery and jalapeño and cook until just tender, another 3 or 4 minutes. Stir in curry paste until fragrant, for about 30 seconds.

3. Add chicken broth, coconut milk, red pepper and cabbage and bring to a simmer. Cook for about 10 minutes.

4. Add cod chunks, shrimp, and calamari and continue to simmer until fish is cooked through, for about 5 to 10 minutes more.

5. Remove from heat and stir in fish sauce and lime juice. Add fresh cilantro just before serving.

6. Serve and enjoy!

## Hazelnut Crusted Sea Bass

Preparation time: 15 minutes

Cooking time: 15 minutes

Overall time: 30 minutes

Serves: 2 to 3 people

**Recipe Ingredients:**

- 2 tablespoons butter
- 1/3 cup of toasted hazelnuts
- ½ teaspoon of salt
- ½ teaspoon of pepper
- ½ teaspoon of garlic powder
- 1/8 teaspoon of cayenne
- 2 Sea bass filet
- Salt and pepper
- 2 slices of lemon
- 1 tablespoon of chopped parsley

**Cooking Instructions:**

1. Preheat oven to 425ºF and place butter in a 9x13 glass or ceramic baking dish. Place the dish in the oven to melt the butter.

2. Meanwhile, combine hazelnuts, salt, pepper, garlic powder, and cayenne in a food processor. Pulse until mixture resembles coarse crumbs with a few bigger pieces of hazelnut.

3. When the butter is melted and bubbly, remove from the oven. Pat the sea bass dry with paper towels and lay them, skin-side down, in the pan.

4. Spoon some of the melted butter from the pan over the filets. Sprinkle with salt and pepper. Sprinkle with the filets with the hazelnut mixture, pressing lightly to adhere.

5. Squeeze the lemon slices over the fish and then lay the slices on top. Bake for about 12 to 15 minutes, until fish is no longer opaque and flakes easily with a fork.

6. Remove and sprinkle with chopped parsley. Spoon the butter from the bottom of the dish onto the filets after you plate them. Serve and enjoy!

## Buttered Cod in Skillet

Preparation time: 5 minutes

Cooking time: 5 minutes

Overall time: 10 minutes

Serves: 2 to 4 people

**Recipe Ingredients:**

**Cod:**

- 1 1/2 pounds of cod fillets
- 6 tablespoons of unsalted butter, sliced

**Seasoning:**

- ¼ teaspoon of garlic powder
- ½ teaspoon of table salt
- ¼ teaspoon of ground pepper
- ¾ teaspoon of ground paprika
- Few lemon slices
- Herbs, parsley or cilantro

**Cooking Instructions:**

1. Stir together ingredients for seasoning in a small bowl. Cut cod into smaller pieces, if desired. Season all sides of the cod with the seasoning.

2. Heat 2 tablespoons butter in a large skillet over medium-high heat. Once butter melts, add cod to skillet. Cook for about 2 minutes.

3. Turn heat down to medium. Turn cod over, top with remaining butter and cook another 3 to 4 minutes. Butter will completely melt and the fish will cook.

4. Don't overcook the cod, it will become mushy and completely fall apart. Drizzle cod with fresh lemon juice. Top with fresh herbs, if desired.

5. Serve immediately and enjoy!

## Fried Fish

Preparation time: 10 minutes

Cooking time: 15 minutes

Overall time: 25 minutes

Serves: 2 to 4 people

**Recipe Ingredients:**

- 1 pound White Fish cod, tilapia, or Pollock
- ¾ cup Almond Flour
- Salt and pepper
- 2 to 3 teaspoon of paprika
- 2 eggs, beaten
- Oil for frying

**Cooking Instructions:**

1. Heat the oil over medium high heat a heavy skillet. If you have an electric skillet, set it to 375ºF and set up the well beaten eggs in a rectangular dish.

2. Then combine the almond meal, and Tony's (or other seasoning) and place on a plate or shallow dish for dipping the fish.

3. Using paper towels, pat the fish very dry, then season both sides with salt and pepper dip in the egg.

4. Then coat both sides in the almond flour mixture – shaking to remove the excess. Place the fish into the hot oil in the skillet.

5. Allow to cook for about 2 to 4 minutes per side, depending upon the thickness of your fish. Remove to a platter, and allow to cool slightly before serving.

6. Serve and enjoy!

## Tuna Melts

Preparation time: 10 minutes

Cooking time: 15 minutes

Overall time: 25 minutes

Serves: 1 to 3 people

**Recipe Ingredients:**

- 2 large tomatoes
- 1 can of flaked light tuna in water
- 2 tablespoons of mayo
- 2 to 4 tablespoons of green onion chopped
- 1/2 cup cheddar cheese or whatever cheese you like
- 2 pickles sliced
- 4 pieces of bacon cooked
- 4 slices of avocado
- Salt and pepper to taste

**Cooking Instructions:**

1. Heat your oven to 400°F and slice the tomato in half and scoop out the seeds. You don't have to do this, but if you leave the seeds in, it can get runny.

2. Open the can of tuna, scoop it into a bowl, add the mayo and the green onion. Stir to combine. Place the tomatoes on a parchment lined baking sheet.

3. Put half the tuna mix on each tomato half. Top each tomato half with pickle slices and then the cheese.

4. Bake in the oven for about 15 minutes or until cheese is melted and bubbly. Remove from the oven and serve right away.

# VEGETERIAN & VEGAN RECIPES

## Smoothie Bowl

Preparation time: 5 days 10 minutes

Cooking time: 15 minutes

Gross time: 5 days 10 minutes

Serves: 10 people

**Recipe Ingredients:**

- ½ cup of frozen cauliflower
- ½ cup of frozen zucchini
- 1 cup of frozen spinach loosely packed
- 1 cup of frozen blueberries preferably wild
- 1 cup of milk alternative (try homemade hemp-milk)
- 2 tablespoons of almond butter (or peanut butter)
- 3 tablespoons of hemp hearts
- 1 teaspoon of cinnamon ground

**Optional Toppings:**

- Hemp hearts
- Berries fresh or frozen
- Granola (grain-free for low-carb)

**Cooking Instructions:**

1. This smoothie bowl works best with frozen cauliflower and zucchini. Frozen spinach is easy to have on hand, but fresh works fine as well.

2. Add all of the ingredients into a high-speed blender, starting with the frozen ingredients closest to the blade.

3. Blend until a creamy consistency is achieved and all the ingredients are well incorporated. Divide the banana-free smoothie bowl mix into two bowls.

4. Top with homemade granola, fresh fruit, and additional hemp hearts. Serve immediately and Enjoy!

## Maple Oatmeal

Preparation time: 5 minute

Cooking time: 20 minutes

Overall time: 25 minutes

Serves: 2 to 4 people

**Recipe Ingredients:**

- ½ cup (60 g) of walnuts
- ½ cup (60 g) pecans
- ¼ cup (40 g) of sunflower seeds
- ¼ cup of coconut flakes
- 1000ml of unsweetened almond milk
- 4 tablespoons of chia seeds
- 3/8 teaspoon of stevia powder
- ½ teaspoon of cinnamon
- 1 teaspoon of maple flavoring (optional)

**Cooking Instructions:**

1. Add the walnuts, pecans and sunflower seeds to a food processor and pulse a few times to crumble them up.

2. In a large pot, add all of the ingredients. Put on low and simmer for a good 20 to 30 minutes, stirring, until the chia seeds have absorbed most of the liquid.

3. Don't forget to stir as the seeds can stick to your pot at the bottom. When the oatmeal has thickened, turn off the heat and serve hot.

4. You can also let it cool down and store it in the fridge for your breakfast the next day. Serve with fresh fruits and any other desired toppings.

## Keto Guacamole

Preparation time: 5 minutes

Cooking time: 10 minutes

Total time: 15 minutes

Serve: 2 to 4 people

**Recipe Ingredients:**

- 3 avocados, ripe
- ½ small onion, finely diced
- 2 Roma tomatoes, diced
- 3 tablespoons of fresh cilantro, chopped
- 1 jalapeno pepper, seeds removed and finely diced
- 2 garlic cloves, minced
- 1 lime, juiced
- ½ teaspoon of sea salt

**Cooking Instructions:**

1. Slice the avocados in half, remove the pit and skin and place in a mixing bowl.

2. Mash the avocado with a fork and make it as chunky or smooth as you'd like.

3. Add the remaining ingredients and stir together.

4. Serve immediately and Enjoy!

## Low Carb Crackers

Preparation time: 10 minutes

Cooking time: 15 minutes

Gross time: 25 minutes

Serves: 4 to 6 people

**Recipe Ingredients:**

- 1 cup of almond flour
- 2 tbsp. of sunflower seeds
- 1 tbsp. of whole psyllium husks or flax meal
- ¾ tsp. of sea salt to taste
- 2 tbsp. of water
- 1 tbsp. of coconut oil

**Cooking Instructions:**

1. Preheat oven to 350°F and blend together almond flour, sunflower seeds, psyllium, and sea salt in bowl or food processor.

2. If using food processor, pulse in water and coconut oil until dough forms. If blending by hand, stir the liquid ingredients into dry ingredients to form dough.

3. Place dough ball on a sheet of parchment paper and press flat. Cover with another sheet of parchment paper and roll dough to about 1/8 to 1/16-inch thickness.

4. Put on cutting board, remove top parchment paper, and cut into 1-inch squares using a pizza cutter or knife. Sprinkle sea salt on top if desired.

5. Place cut dough on a baking sheet and bake in 350°F until edges are brown and crisp (about 10 to 15 minutes).

6. Allow to cool on a rack then separate into squares. Serve immediately and Enjoy!

Avocado Arugula Tomato Salad

Preparation time: 5 minutes

Cooking time: 15 minutes

Gross time: 20 minutes

Serves: 2 to 4 people

**Recipe Ingredients:**

**Tomato Salad:**

- 1 pint of yellow cherry or grape tomatoes, sliced in half
- 1 pint of red cherry or grape tomatoes, sliced in half
- 5 ounces of baby arugula, roughly chopped
- 2 large firm avocados (ripe but not too soft), cut into chunks
- ¼ cup of red onion, diced
- 6 large basil leaves, thinly sliced

**Balsamic Vinaigrette:**

- 2 tablespoon of balsamic vinegar
- 1 tablespoon of olive oil
- 1 tablespoon of maple syrup
- 1 tablespoon of lemon juice
- 1 garlic clove, minced
- ½ teaspoon of Italian seasonings
- ¼ teaspoon of pink sea salt
- ¼ teaspoon of pepper

**Cooking Instructions:**

1. Put the halved tomatoes, chopped arugula, diced red onion, basil leaves, and avocado chunks into a large mixing bowl.

2. In a small bowl, whisk the vinegar, olive oil, maple syrup, lemon juice, garlic, Italian seasonings, salt, and pepper until well combined.

3. Pour the dressing over the tomato salad. Gently mix the salad until the dressing has been evenly distributed.

4. Garnish with fresh basil and serve.

## Triple Green Kale Salad

Preparation time: 5 minutes

Cooking time: 10 minutes

Overall time: 15 minutes

Serves: 2 to 4 people

**Recipe Ingredients:**

**Section 1:**

- 8 to 10 ounces of Lacinato kale, aka tuscan kale, slice to small pieces
- 2 teaspoon of toasted sesame oil
- 2 teaspoon of extra virgin olive oil, alt. flaxseed oil
- 2 small garlic cloves, grated or crushed
- 1 teaspoon of grated fresh ginger
- Pinch of coarse sea salt

**Section 2:**

- Snow peas, chopped, large handful
- 2 teaspoons of coconut aminos
- 2 teaspoon of aged balsamic vinegar
- 1 ripe avocado, sliced
- Scallions, chopped, small handful
- Orange zest, use a microplane
- Sprinkle with hemp seeds, as much as you like

**Cooking Instructions:**

1. Rinse and wash the kale thoughtfully. Pat dry. Lay a kale leaf on a cutting board and run a paring knife along each side of the center stem.

2. Repeat until all the stems have been removed. Stack 4-5 layers of kale leaves and roll them up to slice into smaller pieces.

3. Combine chopped kale leaves with all the ingredients under "Section 1". Use clean hands to gently massage the kale, rubbing the oil into the leaves for a few seconds.

4. Add "Part 2" of the ingredients. Give a quick toss and serve in room temperature or slightly chilled.

5. Serve immediately and Enjoy!

Tomato Mushroom Spaghetti Squash

Preparation time: 30 minutes

Cooking time: 10 minutes

Gross time: 40 minutes

Serves: 2 to 4 people

**Recipe Ingredients:**

- 2 spaghetti squash cooked "al dente", about 6 cups.
- 2 cups of diced tomatoes
- 4 cloves of garlic minced
- 8 oz. of mushrooms sliced
- 1/3 cup of chopped onions or shallots
- ¼ cup of toasted pine nuts
- Small handful of fresh basil cut chiffonade
- 3 tbsp. of olive oil
- Kosher salt and black pepper to taste
- Pinch of red pepper flakes if desired
- Optional: Parmesan cheese

**Cooking Instructions:**

1. Cook spaghetti squash. When cool enough to handle, slice in half, remove seeds and stringy bits and shred with 2 forks.

2. Set the squash aside. In a large Sauté pan, heat oil over medium heat. Add onions and mushrooms, stirring constantly, for about 3 to 4 minutes.

3. Add garlic and stir another minute or 2, just until fragrant. Don't let garlic brown. Add tomatoes and continue stirring.

4. Add cooked spaghetti squash and toss until squash is hot and vegetables are evenly distributed. Toss with fresh basil and toasted pine nuts.

5. Season to taste with kosher salt, pepper and a pinch of red pepper flakes if desired. Serve immediately and Enjoy!

Ginger Asian Slaw

Preparation time: 15 minutes

Cooking time: 1 hour

Gross time: 1 hour 15 minutes

Serves: 6 to 8 people

**Recipe Ingredients**

- 6 cups of thinly sliced green or Napa cabbage (1 small head or 1/2 a medium head)
- 6 cups of thinly sliced red cabbage, (1 small head or 1/2 a medium head)
- 2 cups of shredded carrots
- 1 cup of cilantro, roughly chopped (more to taste)
- ¾ cup of green onions, sliced

**Asian Coleslaw Dressing:**

- 1 tablespoon of olive oil
- 1 tablespoon of maple syrup
- 1 teaspoon of sesame oil
- 1 tablespoon of apple cider vinegar
- 2 tablespoons of tamari
- 1 tablespoon of rice wine vinegar
- 2 tablespoons almond butter
- 1 ½ -inch piece of ginger, grated
- 1 clove of garlic, minced
- ¼ teaspoon of cayenne pepper
- Zest and juice of one medium lime (about 2 to 3 tablespoons of lime juice)
- Sea salt and pepper to taste

**Cooking Instructions:**

1. Put all of the dressing ingredients into a small blender cup and blend until smooth. Put the sliced cabbage, carrots, green onions, and cilantro into a large mixing bowl.

2. Pour the dressing over the cabbage mix and toss to combine. Put the coleslaw in the fridge for at least 1 hour to let the flavors meld. Serve chilled.

## Roasted Cauliflower Soup

Preparation time: 10 minutes

Cooking time: 30 minutes

Gross time: 40 minutes

Serves: 4 to 6 people

**Recipe Ingredients:**

- 1 large cauliflower
- 1 tablespoon of olive oil
- 1 medium yellow onion diced
- 4 ounces of Thai red curry paste (4-5 tbsp)
- 4 cups of vegetable broth (low sodium)
- 14 ounces can of unsweetened coconut milk
- ¼ teaspoon of Himalayan pink sea salt
- 1 tablespoon of lemon juice (about 1/2 a lemon)
- Green onions sliced

**Cooking Instructions:**

1. Preheat the oven to 400°F and cut the florets off the cauliflower and quarter the onion. Lay the cauliflower and onions on a parchment-lined baking tray.

2. Toss in olive oil and bake for about 20 minutes. Add the roasted cauliflower, onions, and vegetable broth to a high-powered blender.

3. Blend until completely smooth and creamy. Pour the cauliflower puree into a soup pot over medium heat.

4. Stir in the coconut milk, red curry paste, salt, and lemon juice. Mix it well and let it cook until hot all the way through.

5. Serve and garnish each bowl with green onions.

## Ginger Cauliflower Fried Rice

Preparation time: 10 minutes

Cooking time: 20 minutes

Overall time: 30 minutes

Serves: 2 to 4 people

**Recipe Ingredients:**

- 1 large head of cauliflower (florets removed)
- 2 tablespoon of coconut oil
- 1 medium onion, diced
- 10 ounces of bag frozen broccoli florets or 1 head of fresh broccoli (florets removed)
- 1 cup of carrot sticks
- 2 to 3 tablespoon of water
- 2 tablespoons of fresh ginger, grated
- 1/3 cup of tamari
- Pepper to taste
- ¼ cup of green onions (thinly sliced)
- ½ cup of fresh cilantro (roughly chopped)

**Cooking Instructions:**

1. Cut the cauliflower florets off and put them into the food processor and pulse on high until it resembles small rice grains and set aside.

2. Sauté the diced onions in coconut oil in a large pan over medium heat until softened. Add the frozen broccoli, carrot sticks and water.

3. Cover and let the water steam the vegetables until soft. Remove the lid and push the veggies to one side of the pan.

4. Add the cauliflower rice, fresh ginger, and tamari to the other side of the pan. Stir to combine. Cook for about 5 minutes or until cauliflower rice is cooked through.

5. Season with pepper. Garnish with cilantro and green onions.

## Garlic Roasted Radishes

Preparation time: 5 minutes

Cooking time: 30 minutes

Gross time: 35 minutes

Serves: 4 to 6 people

**Recipe Ingredients**

- 3 radish bunches (about 20-25 radishes)
- ½ cup of low-sodium vegetable broth
- 3 garlic cloves minced
- ½ teaspoon of dried rosemary
- ½ teaspoon of onion powder
- ¼ teaspoon of oregano
- Himalayan pink sea salt and pepper to taste
- 1 teaspoon of fresh rosemary (optional)

**Cooking Instructions:**

1. Preheat the oven to 400°F and prepare the radishes by cutting off the stems, greens, and roots, rinse them well.

2. Then cut each radish in half. If the radishes are much bigger than a quarter you will want to quarter them so they cook quicker.

3. In a medium-sized casserole or baking dish, add the vegetable broth, minced garlic, rosemary, onion powder, oregano, salt, and pepper.

4. Whisk it well to combine. Add all of the radishes to the baking dish, spoon the broth over the radishes to coat each one.

5. Bake it for about 30 to 35 minutes. Check the radishes at 25 minutes if they are on the small side or until the radishes are tender, stirring halfway through.

6. Garnish with fresh rosemary and serve!

## Roasted Cabbage with Lemon

Preparation time: 5 minutes

Cooking time: 25 minutes

Overall time: 30 minutes

Serves: 2 to 4 people

**Recipe Ingredients:**

- 1 large head of green cabbage
- 2 tablespoon of olive oil
- 2-3 tablespoons of fresh squeezed lemon juice
- Generous amount of sea salt and fresh ground black pepper
- Lemon slices, for serving cabbage (optional)

**Cooking Instructions:**

1. Preheat oven to 450°F. Spray a roasting pan with non-stick spray or olive oil.

2. Cut the head of cabbage into 8 same-size wedges, cutting through the core and stem end. Arrange wedges in a single layer on the roasting pan.

3. Whisk together the olive oil and lemon juice. Then use a pastry brush to brush the top sides of each cabbage wedge with the mixture.

4. Season generously with salt and fresh ground black pepper. Turn cabbage wedges carefully, then brush the second side with the olive oil/lemon juice mixture.

5. Season with salt and pepper. Roast cabbage for about 15 minutes, or until the side touching the pan is nicely browned.

6. Then remove pan from oven turn each wedge carefully. Put back into oven and roast 10-15 minutes more, until the cabbage is nicely browned.

7. Cooked through with a bit of chewiness remaining. Serve hot, with additional lemon slices to squeeze lemon juice on at the table if desired.

Garlic Aioli

Preparation time: 5 minutes

Cooking time: 30 minutes

Overall time: 35 minutes

Serves: 6 to 8 people

**Recipe Ingredients:**

- ¾ cup of Vegenaise
- 3 fresh garlic cloves, minced
- 2 ½ tablespoon of fresh lemon juice
- ¼ teaspoon of pink sea salt (or more to taste)
- ¼ teaspoon of black pepper

**Cooking Instructions:**

1. Add all ingredients to a bowl and whisk to combine. Cover and refrigerate for about 30 minutes.

2. Serve immediately and Enjoy.

## Homemade Vegan Ranch

Preparation time: 10 minutes

Cooking time: 10 minutes

Gross time: 20 minutes

Serves: 6 to 8 people

**Recipe Ingredients:**

- 1 ½ cups of raw cashew pieces
- ¾ cup of water
- 2 tbsp. of rice vinegar
- Juice from 1 large lemon
- 1 tsp. of salt
- 1 ½ tsp. of garlic powder
- 1 ½ tsp. of onion powder
- ¼ cup of fresh dill OR 2-3 teaspoons dried dill

**Cooking Instructions:**

1. Soak the raw cashew pieces in hot water for 5 to 10 minutes. Heat up water in my electric kettle and pour it over the cashews to soak.

2. Drain the cashews and add to your blender. Add the remaining ingredients except the dill, and blend until very smooth.

3. Add the dill, and pulse a few times to combine. You don't want to blend the dill or it will end up very green. Serve on salad or with fresh vegetables for dipping.

4. This will keep for up to a week in the fridge. It will thicken in the fridge, just thin out with water until it reaches the consistency you prefer.

## Basil Pesto

Preparation time: 3 minutes

Cooking time: 2 minutes

Overall time: 5 minutes

Serves: 4 to 6 people

**Recipe Ingredients:**

- 1 large clove of garlic peeled
- 2 cups of fresh organic basil leaves packed
- 1/3 cup of extra virgin olive oil
- 1/3 cup of toasted pine nuts or walnuts
- 1 tbsp. of nutritional yeast optional but highly recommended
- Sea salt and pepper

**Cooking Instructions:**

1. Place garlic in processor or blender and pulse until chopped. Add all other ingredients and process until almost smooth.

2. Toss with pasta, zoodles, roasted potatoes or use to top steak, chicken, or salmon.

3. Serve immediately and Enjoy!

## Chocolate Almond Avocado Pudding

Preparation time: 5 minutes

Cooking time: 5 minutes

Overall time: 10 minutes

Serves: 1 to 3 people

### Recipe Ingredients:

- 1 ½ cups of almond milk
- ½ cup of coconut cream
- 3 tbsp. of granulated stevia
- 1 medium avocado peeled and pitted
- 3 tbsp. of unsweetened cocoa powder
- 1 tsp. of vanilla extract
- 1 tsp. of almond extract
- Unsweetened coconut flakes for garnish (optional)
- Sliced almonds for garnish (optional)

### Cooking Instructions

1. Place all ingredients in a blender and blend until smooth. Pour into serving sized cups and cover

2. Refrigerate for at least 5 hours or preferably overnight.

3. Garnish with unsweetened coconut flakes and sliced almonds just before serving.

# APPETIZER RECIPES

### Veggie Dip

Preparation time: 5 minutes

Cooking time: 5 minutes

Gross time: 10 minutes

Serves: 2 to 4 people

**Recipe Ingredients:**

- 150 grams of soft goat cheese
- 1/3 cup of mayonnaise
- 2 tbsp. of lemon juice
- 1 tbsp. of mixed Mediterranean dried herbs: oregano, garlic, rosemary, and thyme
- Sea salt and freshly ground pepper, to taste

**Cooking Instructions:**

1. Begin by mashing the goat cheese with a fork, in a medium-sized bowl. Once mashed, add mayonnaise and lemon juice.

2. Drop in dried herbs and stir to combined. Serve with a large veggie tray for a healthy snack.

## Chicken Wings

Preparation time: 5 minutes

Cooking time: 40 minutes

Overall time: 45 minutes

Serves: 1 to 3 people

**Recipe Ingredients:**

- 2 lb. of chicken wing segments (flats and drums) 700 grams
- 2 tablespoons of Olive oil
- 3 teaspoons of Adobo seasoning

**Cooking Instructions:**

1. Preheat oven to 390°F and line a baking tray with foil and then place a cooling rack inside the baking tray.

2. In a small bowl combine the olive oil and the seasoning and stir till combine. Pat the chicken wing segments dry with some paper towel.

3. Place them in a large bowl and pour the seasoned olive oil over the chicken segments and toss until they are all completely coated.

4. We find this is easiest using our hands. Place the wings on the rack over the tray, space them evenly so the air can circulate around them.

5. Place in the oven for about 40 to 45 minutes until they are golden brown and the skin is crispy.

6. Serve with your favorite Keto dipping sauce and Enjoy!

## Macadamia Nut Hummus

Preparation time: 5 minutes

Cooking time: 5 minutes

Gross time: 10 minutes

Serves: 6 to 8 people

**Recipe Ingredients:**

- 1 cup of raw macadamia nuts, soaked in water for 24 hours, drained and rinsed
- 3 cloves of garlic
- 3 tbsp. of fresh lemon juice
- 3 tbsp. of water
- 2 tbsp. of tahini
- Pinch cayenne pepper
- Sea salt and freshly ground pepper, to taste

**Cooking Instructions:**

1. Add all ingredients to the bowl of your food processor or high powered blender and blend on high until smooth.

2. Serve immediately and Enjoy!

## Spicy Cheese Crisps

Preparation time: 5 minutes

Cooking time: 10 minutes

Overall time: 15 minutes

Serves: 10 to 12 minutes

**Recipe Ingredients:**

- Grass-fed cheddar cheese
- 1 medium sized jalapeno
- 2 slices of bacon

**Cooking Instructions:**

1. Preheat oven to 425 degrees and line a baking sheet with parchment paper. Add even heaped tablespoons of cheese to prepared baking sheet.

2. Place one slice of jalapeño in the center of mound. Sprinkle with crumbled bacon. Bake on high for about 7 to 10 minutes until cheese is melted.

3. Remove from oven and let cool completely until crisp. Serve immediately and Enjoy!

Antipasto Kebabs

Preparation time: 5 minutes

Cooking time: 5 minutes

Gross time: 10 minutes

Serves: 2 to 4 people

**Recipe Ingredients:**

- Baby heirloom tomatoes
- Marinated artichoke hearts
- Spanish queen green olives
- Kalamata olives
- Marinated fresh mozzarella balls
- Pepperoncini's
- Salami, sliced
- Other optional ingredients: cubed sharp cheddar cheese, pepperoni, prosciutto, marinated mushrooms, roasted red peppers

**Cooking Instructions:**

1. Thread the ingredients onto the skewers in an alternating fashion until smooth.

2. Serve immediately and Enjoy!

## Jalapeno Poppers

Preparation time: 10 minutes

Cooking time: 20 minutes

Overall time: 30 minutes

Serves: 2 to 4 people

**Recipe Ingredients:**

- 8 ounces of cream cheese
- ½ cup of shredded sharp cheddar cheese
- 1 teaspoon of pink Himalayan salt
- ½ teaspoon of black pepper
- 8 jalapenos, halved, de-seeded
- 8 slices of bacon, cut in half

**Cooking Instructions:**

1. Preheat oven to 375ºF and line baking sheet with parchment paper. Place bacon slices on paper towel-lined plate and microwave for about 3 minutes.

2. Set aside to slightly cool. In a medium bowl, add cream cheese, shredded sharp cheddar, salt, and pepper and microwave for about 15 seconds.

3. Stir together. Carefully scoop cream cheese mixture into plastic baggie. With a scissors, snip off corner of baggie and pipe contents into jalapenos.

4. Wrap bacon slices around jalapenos and pin with toothpick. Place jalapenos on prepared baking sheet and bake for about 15 minutes.

5. Increase oven heat to broil and broil for about 2 to 3 minutes, watching to ensure cream cheese does not burn.

6. Remove from oven and allow to cool slightly before serving.

## Keto Meatballs

Preparation time: 5 minutes

Cooking time: 20 minutes

Overall time: 25 minutes

Serves: 8 to 10 people

**Recipe Ingredients:**

- 1-pound ground beef
- 1 large egg
- ½ cup grated parmesan
- ½ cup shredded mozzarella
- 1 tablespoon of minced garlic
- 1 teaspoon of black pepper
- ½ teaspoon of salt

**Cooking Instructions:**

1. Preheat oven to 400°F and line baking sheet with parchment paper.

2. In a mixing bowl, using hands, combine all ingredients and knead together until well-incorporated.

3. Form mixture into equal-sized meatballs and place on prepared baking sheet. Bake for about 18-20 minutes.

4. Allow to cool slightly and serve warm.

## Brown Butter Buffalo Bites

Preparation time: 10 minutes

Cooking time: 20 minutes

Overall time: 30 minutes

Serves: 1 to 3 people

**Recipe Ingredients:**

- 1 head of cauliflower (approximately 3 cups of florets)
- ¼ cup of frank's red hot
- 2 tbsp. grass fed butter
- 2 garlic cloves
- Pinch of salt

**Cooking Instructions:**

1. In a small skillet on medium heat, melt the butter. Bring to a simmer until browned. In that time, but your cauliflower into florets.

2. Add to a large bowl. Pre-heat oven to 400°F. Mince the garlic and add it to the butter, it should be almost ready.

3. When the butter is browned, remove it and pour it over the cauliflower. Make sure to get in the garlic cloves.

4. Add in the hot sauce and gently toss to coat. Use tongs to move the florets to a sheet pan. Place them stem side up.

5. Save the extra sauce remaining in the bowl. Bake the cauliflower for about 20 minutes. Remove from the oven, transfer to a serving dish.

6. Drizzle with remaining sauce. Garnish with crispy bacon and serve.

## Baked Sea Scallops

Preparation time: 20 minutes

Cooking time: 15 minutes

Overall time: 35 minutes

Serves: 8 to 10 people

**Recipe Ingredients:**

- 10 pieces of sea scallops on the half shell 375g each without shell
- 4 cloves of garlic finely chopped
- 2 tbsp. of butter
- 1/3 cup of cheddar cheese Freshly Grated
- ¾ cup of mozzarella
- 1/3 cup of heavy cream
- 1/3 cup of pork rind
- 2 jalapeños, thinly sliced
- 2 lemons juice and slices
- Salt and black Pepper to taste
- Fresh parsley for garnishing
- Hot water for soaking shells

**Cooking Instructions:**

1. Preheat oven at 400°F. Remove scallops from shell. Lightly brush and rinse shell with lemon juice combined with water, to eliminate the fishy odor.

2. Soak in hot water for at least 15 minutes. Wipe shells with kitchen towel and return scallops to shell and sprinkle some salt.

3. In a baking tray lined with foil, bake scallops for 5 minutes. Drain scallop form broth. Opt to set aside for another use or discard. Butter and cheese mixture.

4. In a skillet with low heat, melt butter and sauté garlic until slightly brown. Turn off heat then add cream, cheddar cheese, Jalapeño and black pepper.

5. Stir until cheese melts. Pour ½ Tbsp. of butter and cheese mixture to each scallop on shell, sprinkle grated mozzarella cheese, and add the crushed pork rind.

6. Top with 1 slice of Jalapeño for each. Bake for 8 to 10 minutes until cheese is melted and golden in color.

7. Garnish with fresh parsley. Serve immediately and enjoy!

Broccoli Casserole

Preparation time: 10 minutes

Cooking time: 30 minutes

Overall time: 40 minutes

Serves: 6 to 8 people

**Recipe Ingredients:**

- 4 cups of organic fresh broccoli
- 1 cup of heavy whipping cream
- 1 cup of shredded cheddar jack cheese
- 8 eggs
- 1 tablespoon of salt
- 1 teaspoon of oregano herbs optional
- 1 teaspoon of basil herbs optional
- 1 teaspoon of sesame seasoning blend

**Cooking Instructions:**

1. Steam the broccoli for 3 minutes Place steamed broccoli in a baking dish. In a separate bowl, break 8 eggs.

2. Add one cup of heavy whipping cream. Add one cup of shredded cheddar jack cheese.

3. Add everything but the bagel sesame seasoning blend, herbs, spices and salt. Mix everything together with a whisk or fork.

4. Pour your egg and cheese mixture into baking dish with steamed broccoli.

5. Preheat over to 370°F and bake your Keto casserole for about 25 to 30 minutes.

6. Serve immediately and Enjoy!

## Bacon Wrapped Brussel Sprouts

Preparation time: 15 minutes

Cooking time: 35 minutes

Overall time: 50 minutes

Serves: 10 to 12 people

**Recipe Ingredients:**

- 12 strips of bacon
- 12 medium/large Brussel sprouts
- Pepper, to taste

**Cooking Instructions:**

1. Preheat oven to 375°F and line a baking sheet with tin foil. Then, prepare Brussel sprouts by washing and patting dry with a paper towel.

2. To make bacon wrapped Brussel sprouts. Place a Brussel sprout at the top of a piece of bacon.

3. Roll up Brussel sprout inside of bacon, using the full piece of bacon to wrap, then place on baking sheet. Season with pepper, to taste.

4. Bake at 375°F for about 30 to 35 minutes depending on how crispy you like your bacon.

5. To serve, insert a toothpick into each Brussel sprout. Serve immediately and Enjoy!

## Naruto Rolls

Preparation time: 10 minutes

Cooking time: 30 minutes

Gross time: 40 minutes

Serves: 2 to 4 people

**Recipe Ingredients:**

- 1 long cucumber
- ½ avocado
- 3 slices of raw salmon

**Cooking Instructions:**

1. Peel the cucumber and slice it with vegetable slicer Line the sushi roll on the kitchen board and place cling film on top of it.

2. Place the cucumber slices vertically in a way, that each slice overlaps the other. Slice your avocado.

3. Place it horizontally on cucumber slices, same as making sushi rolls. Add slices of salmon.

4. Roll it the same way like sushi rolls and at the end gently press it and wrap with the cling film to hold the shape together.

5. Place it in the freezer for about 10 to 15 minutes. Once cooled, gently remove cling film and with a sharp knife cut the slices.

6. You can add whatever you desire and can serve it with wasabi, caviar. Serve immediately and Enjoy!

## Crab Cake

Preparation time: 5 minutes

Cooking time: 20 minutes

Overall time: 25 minutes

Serves: 2 to 4 people

**Recipe Ingredients:**

- 8 oz. of wild-caught Dungeness crab meat, or any jumbo lump crab meat
- ¼ cup of avocado mayo (try this recipe)
- 1 egg
- ½ tbsp. of Dijon mustard
- 1 tsp. of coconut aminos
- ½ tsp. of fish sauce
- 1 tsp. of apple cider vinegar
- ¼ cup of grated cauliflower
- 4 tbsp. of avocado oil or grass-fed ghee
- 1 tbsp. of green banana flour
- Lemon wedges for serving

**Cooking Instructions:**

1. In a medium-sized bowl, mix all ingredients except avocado oil together. Carefully fold the mixture to evenly distribute ingredients.

2. In a medium skillet over medium heat, add avocado oil or ghee and heat until shimmering.

3. Using a 1/3 measuring cup, scoop up part of the crab mixture to mold into a cake. Avoid packing the mixture down too tightly.

4. Add crab cake to the pan and repeat with the remainder of the base. Cook crab cakes for about 2 to 3 minutes per side, or until slightly golden on each side.

5. Serve warm with a green salad and lemon wedges.

## Roasted Salt & Pepper Radish Chips

Preparation time: 10 minutes

Cooking time: 15 minutes

Overall time: 25 minutes

Serves: 2 to 4 people

**Recipe Ingredients:**

- 16 oz. of fresh radishes
- 2 tablespoons of coconut oil melted or olive oil
- ½ teaspoon of sea salt
- ½ teaspoon of pepper

**Cooking Instructions:**

1. Preheat oven to 400°F and thinly slice radishes or use a mandolin, place in a bowl. Toss with oil.

2. Lay radishes onto two baking sheets, don't overlap. Whisk the salt and pepper together then sprinkle over the slices.

3. Bake for about 12 to 15 minutes and serve.

Black Olive Tapenade

Preparation time: 5 minutes

Cooking time: 5 minutes

Gross time: 10 minutes

Serves: 6 to 8 people

**Recipe Ingredients:**

- 1 cup of black olives cured in brine
- 1/8 cup of capers
- ½ cup cold-pressed, high-quality extra virgin olive oil
- 2 garlic cloves
- 3 tbsp. of lemon juice
- 2 tsp. of apple cider vinegar
- 1 cup of fresh basil
- 1 cup of fresh parsley
- ½ tsp. of black pepper

**Cooking Instructions:**

1. Place all ingredients into a blender or food processor and blend on low until all is well combined, though not completely smooth.

2. Pour into a glass container and store in your fridge for up to 1 week, or serve immediately with vegetable crudités or grain-free crackers.

3. Serve immediately and Enjoy!

## Cucumber Salsa

Preparation time: 5 minutes

Cooking time: 10 minutes

Gross time: 15 minutes

Serves: 10 to 18 people

**Recipe Ingredients:**

- 2 medium cucumbers peeled, seeded, and chopped (about 2 1/2 cups)
- 2 medium tomatoes chopped (about 1 1/2 cups)
- 4 medium jalapeño peppers seeded and chopped
- ½ medium red onion chopped
- 1 clove of garlic minced
- 2 tbsp. of lime juice
- 2 tsp. of fresh parsley finely chopped
- 2 tsp. of fresh cilantro finely chopped
- ½ tsp. of salt

**Cooking Instructions:**

1. Combine all ingredients in large bowl.
2. Serve with low carb tortilla chips and Enjoy!

Creamy Avocado Sauce

Preparation time: 5 minutes

Cooking time: 5 minutes

Gross time: 10 minutes

Serves: 6 to 8 people

**Recipe Ingredients:**

- 1 avocado — halved, seeded and peeled
- ¼ cup chopped fresh parsley leaves
- 3 tbsp. of olive oil
- 1 small garlic clove
- 1 tbsp. of freshly squeezed lime juice
- Kosher salt and freshly ground black pepper — to taste

**Cooking Instructions:**

1. In a food processor, add all the ingredients and process until smooth. Taste and adjust seasoning.

2. Use this sauce on top of salads, roasted veggies, fish, chicken and veggie noodles. Serve immediately and Enjoy!

# DESSERT RECIPES

### Blueberry Cupcakes

Preparation time: 10 minutes

Cooking time: 16 minutes

Overall time: 26 minutes

Serves: 10 to 12 people

**Recipe Ingredients:**

- 110g of butter melted
- 4 tablespoons of granulated sweetener of choice or more to taste
- 50g of coconut flour
- 1 teaspoon of baking powder
- 1 teaspoon of vanilla
- 2 tablespoons of lemon juice
- 2 tablespoons of lemon zest
- 8 eggs - medium
- 120g of fresh blueberries

**Cooking Instructions:**

1. Mix the melted butter, sweetener, coconut flour, baking powder, vanilla, lemon juice and zest together. Add the eggs, one at a time, mixing between each addition.

2. Taste the cupcake batter to ensure you have used enough sweetener and flavors to mask the subtle taste of coconut from the coconut flour.

3. Divide the mixture between 12 cupcake cases. Press in a few fresh blueberries in the batter of each cupcake.

4. Bake at 350°F for about 15 minutes, or until golden on the outside, and cooked in the center. Ovens will vary so test as the cupcakes are baking.

5. Cover with sugar-free cream cheese frosting. Vanilla or lemon flavor is perfect. Garnish with fresh blueberries and lemon zest and serve.

## Flourless Chocolate Cake

Preparation time: 15 minutes

Cooking time: 45 minutes

Gross time: 1 hour

Serves: 10 to 12 people

**Recipe Ingredients:**

- 1/3 cup of water
- ¼ tsp. of salt
- ½ cup of low carb sugar substitute
- 12 oz. of unsweetened baking chocolate
- 2/3 cup of butter or ghee, cut into tablespoon size pieces
- 4 large eggs
- Boiling water

**Cooking Instructions:**

1. Line bottom of 9-inch spring form pan with parchment paper. In small pot, heat water, salt, and Swerve over medium heat until salt and sweetener are dissolved.

2. Melt baking chocolate in double boiler or microwave. Mix melted chocolate and butter in large bowl with electric mixer. Beat in the hot water mixture.

3. Add in egg, one at a time, beating well after adding each. Pour mix into prepared spring form pan. Wrap outside well with foil.

4. Place spring form pan in larger cake pan and add boiling water to the outside pan about 1 inch deep. Bake cake in water bath for about 45 minutes at 350°F.

5. Remove and cool slightly on wire rack. Chill cake overnight in refrigerator. Then remove side of spring form pan.

6. Serve immediately and Enjoy!

## No-Bake Coconut Cookies

Preparation time: 5 minutes

Cooking time: 5 minutes

Gross time: 10 minutes

Serves: 6 to 8 people

**Recipe Ingredients:**

- 3 cups of unsweetened shredded coconut
- 3/8 cup of coconut oil
- ½ cup xylitol (or whatever sweetener you like--see Recipe Notes)
- 2 teaspoon of vanilla
- 3/8 teaspoon of salt (adjust amount as desired)

**Optional Toppings:**

- Homemade Chocolate / Carob Chips (melted for drizzle)
- Coconut shreds
- Finely-chopped nuts

**Cooking Instructions:**

1. Put all ingredients in a food processor or blender. Combine until the mixture is blended and sticks together.

2. If you are using a high-powered blender like a Vitamix, do not turn your machine on high. You will likely end up with Coconut Butter.

3. While it will be delicious, it won't be these no-bake cookies. Remove the mixture from the blender / food processor and form into desired shape.

4. Cut into cute little shapes and make with this little cookie scoop. Decorate with shredded coconut, cocoa or carob powder, crushed nuts, or melted chocolate.

5. They are great just as is but I do think a little coconut sprinkled on top adds a nice touch. Leave to firm up on a plate.

6. They will firm up at room temperature. Serve immediately and Enjoy!

## Coconut Macaroons

Preparation time: 5 minutes

Cooking time: 15 minutes

Gross time: 20 minutes

Serves: 6 to 9 people

**Recipe Ingredients:**

- 1 ½ cups of unsweetened shredded coconut
- 5 tbsp. of birch xylitol
- 1 scoop of Vanilla Collagen Protein Powder
- ½ tsp. of baking powder (aluminum-free)
- ½ teaspoon pure almond extract
- 2 pastured egg whites

**Optional:**

- Unsweetened dark chocolate baking chips
- Chocolate bacon fudge
- Bacon-wrapped herb burgers
- Collagen charcoal beauty elixir recipe
- Keto salted cbd brownies

**Cooking Instructions:**

1. Preheat oven to 325°F and place all of the dry ingredients in a mixing bowl and stir well to evenly mix. Add almond extract and egg whites.

2. Stir well to combine. Use a large spoon to scoop 9 equal servings and place them evenly spread apart on a parchment-lined baking sheet.

3. If unlined, you will need to brush your baking sheet with oil to keep the macaroons from sticking.

4. Top each macaroon with a few unsweetened dark chocolate chips before placing in the oven. Bake for approximately 15 minutes or until macaroons are browned.

5. Using a spatula, remove from baking sheet and allow to cool before eating. Serve and enjoy!

Shortbread Cookies

Preparation time: 20 minutes

Cooking time: 1 hour 10 minutes

Overall time: 1 hour 20 minutes

Serves: 12 to 24 people

**Recipe Ingredients:**

- 1 1/3 cup (145g) of almond flour
- ¼ tsp. of fine sea salt
- 1/3 cup plus 1 teaspoon (80g) of grass-fed butter or ghee
- 4 tbsp. (40g) of erythritol monk fruit blend
- 1/2 tsp. of vanilla extract
- 1 tbsp. (8g) of coconut flour
- 1 tbsp. (8g) collagen peptides
- 1 vanilla shortbread collagen protein bar, crumbled

**Chocolate glaze ingredients (optional):**

- 5 oz. (134g) of quality dark chocolate (at least 85% cacao), chopped
- 3 tbsp. of avocado oil
- 2 scant tbsp. of cacao nibs

**Cooking Instructions:**

1. In a food processor, mix all shortbread ingredients except for the collagen bar until combined.

2. Remove and spread the dough carefully with a rolling pin until it is about 3.5mm thick. Cut out cookies with curly round cutter and freeze for about 30 minutes.

3. Preheat oven to 350°F and prepare a perforated baking tray with parchment or a silicone liner.

4. Remove cookies from the freezer, place on the baking sheet, and bake for about 8 minutes, or until golden.

5. Baking time will vary depending on your oven, baking tray, and cookie thickness. Allow shortbread to cool completely before adding glaze.

6. While cookies cool, prepare the glaze: Using a double boiler on the stovetop, gently melt chocolate and oil together until well combined.

7. Mix in cacao nibs. Drizzle cooled cookies with the chocolate glaze and sprinkle with collagen bar crumbs.

8. Serve and enjoy!

## Coconut Lime Bars

Preparation time: 10 minutes

Cooking time: 50 minutes

Gross time: 60 minutes

Serves: 8 to 10 people

**Recipe Ingredients:**

**Lime Bars Ingredients:**

- 4 cups of desiccated coconut
- 4 tbsp. of coconut oil or ghee
- 4 tbsp. of lime juice (about half a large lime), plus zest
- 6 tbsp. of collagen peptides
- 3 tsp. of vanilla extract, or 2 teaspoons vanilla powder
- 2 tbsp. of MitoSweet or granulated erythritol and monk fruit sweetener
- Pinch of salt

**Matcha Topping Ingredients:**

- ½ cup of coconut cream
- 2 tbsp. of ghee or coconut oil
- 1 tsp. of high-quality matcha
- 1 tbsp. of lime juice
- ½ tbsp. of MitoSweet, or liquid stevia to taste
- 1 tsp. of vanilla extract, or 1/2 teaspoon vanilla powder

**Cooking Instructions:**

1. Prepare the lime bars: In a blender, add desiccated coconut and blitz until fine, stopping to scrape down the sides of the blender as needed.

2. Add all the remaining vanilla slice ingredients except collagen and blend until fine and well-combined.

3. Add collagen, and blend on the lowest setting until just mixed. Taste the mixture and add more lime juice or sweetener if desired.

4. Line a small loaf tin with parchment paper, add the mix, and press down gently with your hands or the back of a spoon until even and compact.

5. Place in the freezer until firm. Prepare the matcha topping. In a saucepan on low heat, add all topping ingredients and melt together.

6. Use a fork or whisk, or blend for a few seconds on medium speed so it combines well. Place the mix in a small bowl, and then into your fridge to set slightly.

7. To serve, cut your lime bars into pieces and scoop the matcha mixture on top.

## Coconut Blondies

Preparation time: 10 minutes

Cooking time: 40 minutes

Overall time: 50 minutes

Serves: 7 to 9 people

**Recipe Ingredients:**

- ½ cup (113g) of butter, unsalted softened
- ½ cup (105g) of erythritol or sugar substitute
- 4 eggs
- ½ cup (56g) of coconut flour
- ¼ cup (56g) of coconut milk
- ½ cup (30g) of desiccated coconut unsweetened
- 1 tbsp. of vanilla extract
- ¼ tsp. of baking powder
- ¼ tsp. of salt

**Cooking Instructions:**

1. Preheat the oven to 350°F and grease and line a 8 inch baking pan with parchment paper.

2. In a bowl, cream the butter and erythritol together until smooth. Add the eggs, mixing into the batter, once at a time.

3. Then, add the vanilla extract and coconut milk and beat until smooth. Add the coconut flour, desiccated coconut, baking powder and salt.

4. Stir until smooth. If the mixture is a bit too thick, add more coconut milk. Spoon into the baking tin and bake for about 25 to 30 minutes until firm and golden.

5. Allow to cool in the tin for at least 30 minutes. Cut into squares and enjoy!

## Chocolate Coconut Bars

Preparation time: 5 minutes

Cooking time: 25 minutes

Gross time: 30 minutes

Serves: 10 to 12 people

**Recipe Ingredients:**

**Bottom Coconut layer:**

- 2 cups of shredded unsweetened coconut
- 1/3 cup of virgin coconut oil, melted
- ¼ cup of granulated eythritol

**Chocolate topping layer:**

- 3 squares of unsweetened chocolate (about 3 ounces of chocolate)
- 1 tbsp. of coconut oil
- 2 tbsp. of nourished sweetener

**Cooking Instructions:**

1. Place shredded coconut, coconut oil and sweetener into a food processor using the S blade.

2. Process until the ingredients form a dough that falls away from the sides, scraping down the sides as needed.

3. Press the coconut mixture into the bottom of a silicone pan, or into 12 molds. Put the pan in the freezer while you prepare the topping.

4. Warm the coconut oil and chocolate at 50% power in microwave until melted. Stir in the sweetener if using unsweetened chocolate.

5. Spread evenly over the frozen coconut layer. Pop back into the freezer for about 30 minutes. Take out of the freezer.

6. Turn the silicone molds inside out to release the frozen contents. These keep very well in a Ziploc in the freezer.

Vanilla Bean Ice Cream

Preparation time: 5 minutes

Cooking time: 20 minutes

Gross time: 25 minutes

Serves: 2 to 4 people

**Recipe Ingredients:**

- 4 pastured eggs
- 4 or 5 pastured egg yolks
- 1 teaspoon of lemon juice or apple cider vinegar
- 100g (7 tablespoons) of grass-fed butter or ghee, melted
- 50g of cacao butter, melted
- 60g (4 tablespoon) of brain octane oil
- 50g of coconut oil, melted
- 50g of sweetener of choice (stevia, xylitol, monk fruit powder etc.)
- 2 tablespoon of filtered water
- 2 teaspoon of vanilla powder

**Cooking Instructions:**

1. Add all the ingredients into a high-powered blender and blitz for about 1 to 2 minutes.

2. Taste the mixture and adjust the sweetness by adding a little more if needed. Pour into an ice-cream maker and churn for about 15 to 20 minutes.

3. Serve and enjoy this incredibly nourishing and delicious ice-cream.

Avocado Popsicles

Prep time: 5 minutes

Cooking time: 25 minutes

Total time: 30 minutes

Serves: 4 to 6 people

**Recipe Ingredients:**

- 2 medium avocados
- 2 tablespoons of lemon juice
- 6 tablespoons of sugar alternative
- 1 cup of unsweetened almond milk

**Chocolate ganache:**

- 80g of low carb chocolate
- 10g of cacao butter

**Cooking Instructions:**

1. Place 2 avocados, lemon juice, and sugar alternative into the mixer and mix properly.

2. Fill all of the molds with the mixture and place it into the freezer to freeze. In the meantime, melt chocolate and Cacao Butter in a double container.

3. Once the Ice pops are frozen, take each one and dip it into the cooled chocolate. The chocolate cannot be too hot, otherwise, it will melt the popsicle as well.

4. Serve immediately and Enjoy!

Frozen Fudge Pops

Preparation time: 5 minutes

Cooking time: 5 minutes

Overall time: 10 minutes

Serves: 2 to 4 people

**Recipe Ingredients:**

- 1 tablespoon of unsweetened chocolate powder
- A pinch of salt
- 2 tablespoon brain octane oil
- 1 teaspoon of vanilla powder
- 270 ml of coconut cream
- 1 tablespoon of cacao butter
- 2 pasture-raised egg yolks
- 2 tablespoons Collagelatin
- Liquid stevia or monk fruit sweetener to taste

**Cooking Instructions:**

1. In a small saucepan add the Brain Octane Oil, Collage Latin, cacao butter, chocolate powder, salt, coconut cream and vanilla and heat on low.

2. Once the mix has come to a soft simmer and all the ingredients have melted and combined together remove from the heat and allow to cool completely.

3. When it has cooled, add the liquid mix, egg yolks, and sweetener to taste to a high powered blender and blitz to combine until smooth and creamy.

4. Pour into ice-block molds and place in the freezer until set. When you're ready to eat them.

5. Run the molds under warm water for a minute or two or until the ice-blocks come away easily from the molds.

6. Enjoy them as they are or simply drizzle melted cacao melts (or dark chocolate) over the top and sprinkle with edible flowers and organic berries.

7. Enjoy immediately!

## Strawberry Ice Cream

Preparation time: 5 minutes

Cooking time: 5 minutes

Gross time: 10 minutes

Serves: 2 to 4 people

**Recipe Ingredients**

- 2 cans (13.5 ounces) of coconut milk
- 16 ounces of frozen strawberries
- 3/4 cup of equivalent sweetener
- ½ cup of chopped fresh strawberries (optional)

**Cooking Instructions:**

1. In a blender combine all the ingredients, except for the fresh strawberries, and blend until smooth.

2. Place the mixture in your ice cream maker and process according to the directions. Add the strawberries right before the ice cream is done to combine.

3. Serve immediately or place the ice cream in the freezer for 1-2 hours to harden.

## Raspberry Lemon

Preparation time: 5 minutes

Cooking time: 5 minutes

Gross time: 10 minutes

Serves: 4 to 6 people

**Recipe Ingredients:**

- 8 oz. of lemon flatwater (1/2 bottle)
- 8 oz. of canned organic coconut cream
- ½ cup of fresh organic raspberries, plus more for garnish if desired
- 1 tbsp. of brain octane oil
- 1 tbsp. of birch xylitol
- Bacon-wrapped herb burgers
- Collagen charcoal beauty elixir recipe
- Keto salted cbd brownies
- 20 low-carb fish recipes you can make in a flash

**Cooking Ingredients:**

1. Place everything in a blender and blend well. Pour into popsicle molds. Makes enough to fill six 4-ounce molds.

2. Add some chunks of fresh raspberries to each mold for garnish. Place lids on popsicle molds and freeze for at least 4 hours.

3. Serve immediately and Enjoy!

Pots De Creme

Preparation time: 5 minutes

Cooking time: 10 minutes

Gross time: 15 minutes

Serves: 2 to 4 people

**Recipe Ingredients:**

- 3 large avocados, skin and pits removed
- 5 tbsp. of cocoa powder
- 1 tsp. of liquid stevia
- ¼ cup of hazelnuts
- 3 oz. of 100% dark chocolate, melted
- Small pinch of salt
- 2 tsp. of vanilla extract
- Optional garnishes: Raw nuts, whipped coconut cream

**Cooking Instructions:**

1. In a food processor, add all ingredients except garnishes. Process pot de crème base until smooth and no chunks of avocado remain.

2. Spoon chocolate paste into small bowls or ramekins. Garnish and enjoy right away for a smoother.

3. Serve immediately and Enjoy!

Chocolate Mousse

Preparation time: 5 minutes

Cooking time 5 minutes

Overall time: 10 minutes

Serves: 4 to 6 people

**Recipe Ingredients:**

- 320ml of coconut milk (or heavy cream for dairy version)
- 150g of unsweetened baking chocolate
- 2 tablespoon of cocoa powder
- 6 tablespoons of powdered erythritol (or approved paleo sweetener)
- 3/8 teaspoon of stevia powder
- 3 eggs

**Cooking Instructions:**

1. Add the coconut milk to a small pot and put to boil. Once boiling, turn off the heat and set aside.

2. Add the unsweetened baking chocolate, cocoa powder, erythritol and stevia powder to a powerful blender.

3. Pulse for about 20 seconds to break the chocolate apart. You want it to just break apart enough so that you don't have huge chocolate parts left.

4. When your chocolate is either all powder or the size of chocolate chips, it's fine. Add the eggs and blend for a minute.

5. You'll now have a thick chocolate cream. Take the small opening off the lid, and while the blender is running, pour the hot milk inside in a slow and steady stream.

6. Don't stop the blender and pour all of the milk in. Let it continue running for another 30 seconds after you've finished adding the cream and that's it.

7. Your chocolate mousse will resemble chocolate liquid. Pour the liquid into 6 different cups, bowls or anything you want to use.

8. Place them in the fridge and let cool for at least 90 minutes or until set. Top with any type of berries you want.

9. Serve and enjoy!

## Coffee Panna Cotta

Preparation time: 5 minutes

Cooking time: 10 minutes

Gross time: 15 minutes

Serves: 1 to 3 people

**Recipe Ingredients:**

- 1 (11-ounce) container of mocha cold-brew bulletproof coffee
- 1 ¾ teaspoons of grass-fed gelatin
- 1 tablespoon of filtered water
- Optional: sweetener, cinnamon, or vanilla to taste
- Optional toppings: chopped or shaved bulletproof chocolate.
- Chocolate bacon fudge
- Bacon-wrapped herb burgers
- Collagen charcoal beauty elixir recipe
- Keto salted cbd brownies

**Cooking Instructions:**

1. In a small saucepan, add the gelatin and water and stir to combine. Set this aside for a minute or two to allow it to 'bloom' and thicken.

2. When the gelatin has bloomed, add in ¼ cup of the cold brew mocha and heat on low until the gelatin has completely dissolved.

3. Now add the remaining cold brew and stir to combine. Remove the pan from heat. Pour the mixture into 2 small glass jars.

4. Place them in the fridge to set, which should take about 1 to 2 hours. When they're ready, serve and enjoy.

## Lemon Coconut Custard Pie

Preparation time: 10 minutes

Cooking time 45 minutes

Overall time 55 minutes

Serves: 6 to 8 people

**Recipe Ingredients:**

- 2 large eggs
- 1 cup of coconut milk canned
- ¾ cup of low carb sugar substitute
- ¼ cup of coconut flour
- 2 tbsp. of unsalted butter melted and cooled
- 1 tsp. of vanilla extract
- ¾ tsp. of baking powder
- 1 tsp. of lemon zest
- ½ tsp. of lemon extract
- 4 oz. of unsweetened shredded coconut

**Cooking Instructions:**

1. Spray a 9-inch pie dish with cooking spray and preheat the oven to 350°F.

2. In a large bowl, mix the eggs, coconut milk, sweetener, coconut flour, butter, baking powder, vanilla, lemon zest, and lemon extract.

3. Stir just until combined. Fold in the unsweetened coconut. Pour the mixture into the pie dish.

4. Bake for about 40 to 45 minutes or until the edges are brown and the top is a light golden brown.

5. Remove from the oven and allow to cool completely before attempting to cut and serve. Store leftovers in the refrigerator for up to three days.

# 21-Day Meal Plan To Lose Up To 20 Pounds In 3 Weeks

| Day | Breakfast | Lunch | Dinner | Desserts |
|---|---|---|---|---|
| 1 | Green Smoothie | Cherry Clafoutis | Avocado Egg | Blueberry Cupcakes |
| 2 | Breakfast Pizza | Chia Jam | Cloud Bread Cheese Danish | Vanilla Bean Ice Cream |
| 3 | Frosted Vanilla Blackberry Lemonade | Baked Denver Omelet | Strawberry Scones | Raspberry Lemon |
| 4 | Salted Caramel Smoothie | Pistachio Truffles Fat Bombs | Raspberry Linzer Cookies | Coconut Blondies |
| 5 | Buttery Coconut Flour Waffles | Salmon Stew | Chia Jam | Coconut Lime Bars |
| 6 | Fluffy Almond Flour Pancakes | Cloud Bread Cheese Danish | Cabbage Soup | Shortbread Cookies |
| 7 | Breakfast Pizza | Ground Pork Tacos | Cherry Clafoutis | Avocado Popsicles |
| 8 | Breakfast Egg Crepes | Baked Denver Omelet | Pistachio Truffles Fat Bombs | Blueberry Cupcakes |
| 9 | Buttery Coconut Flour Waffles | Almond Crescent Cookies | Chili Beef | Coffee Panna Cotta |
| 10 | Salted Caramel Smoothie | Raspberry Cheesecake Bars | Cappuccino Muffins | Coconut Blondies |
| 11 | Green Smoothie | Cherry Clafoutis | Chicken Sliders | Frozen Fudge Pops |

| 12 | Fruit-Free Smoothie | Bruschetta Chicken | Ground Pork Tacos | Raspberry Lemon |
| --- | --- | --- | --- | --- |
| 13 | Cinnamon Chocolate Breakfast Smoothie | Pistachio Truffles Fat Bombs | Raspberry Cheesecake Bars | Chocolate Mousse |
| 14 | Buttery Coconut Flour Waffles | Raspberry Linzer Cookies | Baked Denver Omelet | Avocado Popsicles |
| 15 | Fruit-Free Smoothie | Strawberry Scones | Cappuccino Muffins | Blueberry Cupcakes |
| 16 | Breakfast Egg Crepes | Chicken Sliders | Avocado Egg | Coffee Panna Cotta |
| 17 | Buttery Coconut Flour Waffles | Cappuccino Muffins | Almond Crescent Cookies | Chocolate Mousse |
| 18 | Frosted Vanilla Blackberry Lemonade | Baked Denver Omelet | Raspberry Cheesecake Bars | Coconut Lime Bars |
| 19 | Fluffy Almond Flour Pancakes | Raspberry Linzer Cookies | Chia Jam | Vanilla Bean Ice Cream |
| 20 | Breakfast Pizza | Avocado Egg | Cloud Bread Cheese Danish | Coconut Blondies |
| 21 | Green Smoothie | Cherry Clafoutis | Strawberry Scones | Blueberry Cupcakes |